Memories

of

Exeter

Part of the

Memories

series

Memories
of
Exeter

Edited by Hazel Harvey

*The Publishers would like to thank the following companies for supporting
the production of this book*

Main Sponsor

EBC Group plc

Exeter Housing Society

Hardinge Machine Tools Limited

Kastner Volvo

Thomas Moore of Exeter Limited

M Sillifant & Sons

West of England School

First published in Great Britain by True North Books Limited
Units 3 - 5 Heathfield Industrial Park
Elland West Yorkshire
HX5 9AE
Tel. 01422 377977
© Copyright: True North Books Limited 2000

ISBN 1 900463 94 6

Text, design and origination by True North Books Limited
Printed and bound by The Amadeus Press Limited

Memories are made of this

High Street in the 1940s

Memories. We all have them: people, places and events, some good and some bad. Our memories of the place where we grew up are usually tucked away in a very special place in our mind. The best are probably connected with our childhood and youth, when we longed to be grown up and paid no attention to adults who told us to enjoy being young, as these were the best years of our lives. We look back now and realise that they were right.

Old photographs bring our memories flooding back - coronations and celebrations; talking pictures, Technicolor and television; the war years, rationing, and the shared hopes and fears which created such a warm community spirit; buying things made of nylon and plastic; fashions which took trouserbottoms and hemlines from drainpipes and mini-skirts to the other extreme; Doris Day, Acker Bilk, Elvis Presley and the Beatles; the jitterbug, the tango and discos; Ford Populars and Minis; decimalisation. Life changed so much over the years.

Some changes were big, some small; some altered our lives in ways we never anticipated. Who in the early days of motoring could have foreseen the motorways and traffic systems of the latter decades of the 20th century? Did any of us realise, when we first saw a computer, what a tremendous impact they would have on our lives? Self-service supermarkets and frozen food made our lives easier - but at the expense of our friendly little corner shops. Nostalgia is always such a mixture of feelings . . . We hope that the collection of pictures in this book will remind you of happy days in bygone eras - and who knows, you might even have been there when one of the photographs was taken!

Contents

Exeter through the years

Nothing ever stays the same, and we cannot progress without change. Some changes, however, hurt more than others. The first, still remembered and mourned by many older residents of Exeter, was the clearance scheme of the 1930s which wiped out the West Quarter community. The second had nothing to do with the Planning Department; it was the Luftwaffe who carried out the wholesale destruction of the city centre in 1942, when in 19 heartbreaking air raids 265 people were killed and three-quarters of Exeter's main shopping area was left in smouldering ruins.

Exeter, one of England's most ancient cities, was to rise, like the fabled phoenix, from the ashes - though in a vastly changed form. The new style of architecture was stark and angular, and as the 1950s progressed to the 60s many were to react against the characterless 'square box' buildings that were replacing the old shops, banks,

The day the River Exe burst its banks - 27th October 1960.

pubs and churches - many of which had been architectural gems. Exeter had led the way in pedestrianisation as early as 1949 with Princesshay, but further developments were yet to come as our growing traffic problem demanded an inner bypass, more car parks, traffic-free zones and shopping malls.

We are fortunate that the 20th century was so well chronicled, and this collection of fascinating images call to mind the town as it was in our youth - and long before that! We visit vanished cinemas such as the ABC - formerly the Savoy - where those marvellous Harold Stringer concerts were staged, and the old Empire Electric Palace, which closed before the advent of the talkies, and we take a peep at Deller's, Colson's - and the finest hours of Exeter City FC.

This new collection reproduces these and many more nostalgic images to remind us of the way we once lived. We hope that you will read and enjoy 'Memories of Exeter' - and remember that history is still in the making.

Around the city centre

The new electric tramway system had recently taken over from horses when this photograph was taken; note the line of traction poles along High Street. The buildings themselves changed little between the early days of the 20th century and the second world war. But the fashions! This photograph dates from September 1905, when ladies' 18-inch waistlines were achieved beneath the iron hand of strong corsets, and hemlines swept the ground (how dirty they would get!). The effect was elegance and femininity - but we could also add a note about the shortness of breath, displaced internal organs, and those fainting fits for which the Victorian ladies were famous. Queen Victoria died in 1901, and the Edwardians began to take a healthier view of costume. But what would these very proper ladies and gentlemen have thought if they could have taken a peep into the future, where anything goes, and seen mini-skirted girls, women casting off their corsets and wearing trousers - or worse still, leggings - and horror of horrors, men sporting long hair (or no hair at all) and earrings!

These marvellous merchants' houses have a history which goes back to around 1567. The nearer building became the offices of the old *Flying Post* newspaper, which were destroyed by fire in 1907. A knot of young ladies, all wearing the distinctive dresses and cloche hats of the 1920s, have gathered outside the newspaper offices (note the olde-worlde style lettering which spells out 'Express & Echo' on the frieze above the window), and have found something there to interest them. Further along, posters in the window inform passers-by of the latest news; unfortunately apart from reading that Exeter had a new city engineer, the wording is indecipherable to us. Controversy surrounded the building when C&A gutted the interior, leaving only the facade, removing yet another reminder of Exeter's rich history. The facade still stands today, serving no purpose except ornamentation of the modern fashion store.

Below: Did he catch the tram - or did he miss it? We'll never know - but this would-be passenger chasing the car down Fore Street is giving it his best shot. At least he was running down the road and not up the hill! The steep one in eleven-and-a-half gradient in Fore Street presented a challenge to the tramway system, and this was the scene of a nasty accident back in 1917. We have no date for this photograph, but the style of clothing would indicate the 1930s. The bright early evening sunshine has tempted many out to browse among the shops - yet during the 30s the clouds of war were already hanging low over Britain. These people strolling in Fore Street had no way of knowing of the devastation to come, when bombing raids would wipe out many of the shops at the top end of the street, destroying buildings across a huge area of the city centre.

Bottom: For once, the High Street is reasonably clear of traffic, and there are fewer pedestrians than usual about. A trusting cyclist has left his bicycle leaning against a pole outside the National Provincial; but this was 1928, the gentler days when you could leave your cycle outside a shop doorway and expect to find it still there when you returned. Crimes were certainly committed, but on the whole, people cared more about others back then. Children were taught to respect the local bobby, along with teachers, officers, and anyone else in authority.

The police officer on the right, dressed in a white cape to make him conspicuous, would have been looked up to a good deal more than his equivalent today! Looking westward from London Inn Square, the Exeter Co-operative Society and the Motor Union Insurance Company share a building on the far left; set back from the pavement, between them and the bank, is the entrance to the arcade.

Prominent in this 1918 photograph is the marvellous 'Old Father Time' clock mounted on the wall of Bruford's, Exeter's well-known high class jewellery shop, informing us that this scene of High Street was captured at exactly 11.50 am. It was carved by famous local sculptor, Harry Hems. Further along on the left readers may be able to pick out the ancient church of St Lawrence, built in the 12th century. The church, along with many more of the buildings in central High Street, was to become another victim of the blitz. The nearby Empire Electric Palace was purpose-built as a cinema - Exeter's very

first. For the princely sum of one shilling you could sit in one of the best seats in the house, while if you were down on your luck you could still view the film - though not from so good a seat - for the sum of three-pence. The Empire was opened in August 1910; this, of course, was well before the 'talkies' revolutionised the film industry, and a young lady pianist - still in her teens - had the unenviable task of fitting the music to the on-screen action, whether it was dramatic, romantic or melancholy. The Empire cinema closed in 1937, and the building later fell victim to enemy bombs.

frontage and massive granite columns!

The present Guildhall was built in the 14th century, though we know that a civic building stood on the same spot as early as 1160. Changes, alterations and additions have of course taken place over the years, and each renovation has added its distinctive style to the building. The Mayor's Parlour, supported on those four pillars, was added in the late 16th century. The beautiful carved oak door, unfortunately not visible here, dates from the same period. Much work was carried out in the 19th century, and the Victorian influence characterises a good deal of the interior, especially in the Council Chamber. The timber roof, however, whose major trusses rest on fantastic carved animals, dates from around 1468. Below the roof hangs a magnificent brass chandelier, designed by Thomas Pyke, which was installed in 1789.

Many years ago, the city stocks stood below the portico; a warning to those who might be tempted to stray towards the wrong side of decency and the law - and a punishment to those who did and were caught. Bad eggs, rotten vegetables, and perhaps the odd dead cat, provided a little general entertainment - though the unfortunate man or woman sitting uncomfortably in the stocks would hardly have found it so entertaining!

Both pages: No book about Exeter would be complete without the magnificent Guildhall - probably the oldest civic building in the country and these three views - taken in three different decades, the years of the Great War (1914-1918), the second world war (1939 - 1945), and the 1960s - show us that while the shops, the vehicles and the fashions have all changed, the Guildhall has remained the same, a symbol of stability and permanence. Isn't it amazing, though, how familiarity can breed, if not contempt, at least inattention? Passers-by in the High Street are so used to seeing the Guildhall that they rarely if ever stop to admire the impressive building with its Tudor

This marvellous shot of Exeter High Street, recorded in the early 20th century, reveals a scene which is quite unfamiliar today. Bustling with life and vitality, the camera captures the real character of the city, from the early cars buzzing to and fro to the worker pushing a trolley-load of boxes. To the left of the photograph is Colsons tea lounge and restaurant. The vertical 'Cash Chemists' sign down the side of the Timothy White's building on the corner of Gandy Street is studded with electric light bulbs - in the days when homes were lit by gas, this

illuminated sign would be quite a sight. The windows were rather dull when we compare them with the chemist shops of today, which sparkle with jewellery, hair ornaments, cameras and cosmetics. Timothy Whites, not only a chemists but also a household stores, would later add 'and Taylor' to their name. This was the place to go, not only to have your films developed and your doctor's medicines dispensed but to buy the popular home remedies that had stood the test of time: castor oil, ipecacuanha, camphorated oil, Indian Brandee and Fennings fever powders.

The police constable directing traffic and pedestrians alike was definitely earning his pay on the day this busy scene was caught on camera. High Street was frenetically busy, so much so that the hundreds of people had spilled off the pavements and into the road. Could this really have been a normal shopping day? If so, pedestrianisation was called for in the city many years before it actually arrived. We are tempted to think, though, that a public holiday of some sort is afoot. Dellers confectionery, on the right, would no doubt have had a busy day, as would Webbers, who sold fishing tackle, toys, games, and all kinds of sporting equipment; they later moved to Queen

Street. Any holiday brings out the cameras; in the early 20th century photography was becoming a popular hobby for those who could afford to buy cameras, film and equipment. Kodak was the film to buy at the time - in fact a catchy name for keen photographers was 'Kodakers'. Note the four-legged transport alongside the motor cars; those were the gentler days when the resulting traffic pollution could be put to good use on your floribundas!

CARS, CHAOS AND COST

Britain saw its very first car in 1894. Twenty years later, in 1914, the world's first traffic lights were installed in front of the House of Commons. Cars were here to stay - but they brought with them their own particular problems.

As traffic levels increased in town centres around the country, various schemes were put in place to control the flow. Some involved the motorist's pocket; in 1947 a Road Tax of £1 per year was imposed.

Road safety also became a major issue, and in 1956 the Ministry of Transport introduced road testing, which at first only affected cars more than ten years old.

To the frustration of the many motorists who were used to free parking, parking meters were introduced to Britain in June, 1958. At the same time, yellow no-waiting lines came into force. A whole new way of life began for the British driver.

Bottom: A pleasant sunny day has brought cheerful shoppers out into Exeter High Street, and sun blinds protect the goods on display in well-stocked windows from fading. In spite of the traffic lights placed at the corner of Queen Street a police officer, made conspicuous by his white arm band, keeps a wary eye on motorists and pedestrians alike. A few of the passers-by have become aware of the presence of the camera; having your photograph taken was still quite a novelty at the time, though by the 1930s photography had become a popular pastime - at least among those who could afford the luxury. We have no date for this fascinating image; the elegant Boots building was doomed to fall victim to the red pen of the planners, and the early 1970s were to see C&A on this corner.

Right: A whole new meaning was given to the phrase 'moving house' when plans were made to build Western Way. Laying down the new inner by-pass involved the demolition of those buildings which were unlucky enough to stand in its way. Among them was Number 16 Edmund Street, on the corner of Frog Street and Edmund Street, which was one of Exeter's oldest houses. It was vital that the three-storeyed timbered house, which incredibly dated back to around 1500, be saved, and a hasty preservation order put a stop to any planned demolition. As the new road could not be re-routed, the house itself had to therefore be moved. Modern technology came to the rescue, and between 9th and 12th December 1961 the ancient building was shored up, gingerly lifted on to rollers, and moved 50yds to a new position in West Street. The House that Moved was then fully restored, and went on to became a famous landmark in the city.

Above: Queen Street is busy with traffic and shoppers alike in this pre-war photograph. The new C&A and Marks and Spencer's buildings were to change the view from this point for ever. For the time being, however, people could still buy their dresses, coats, and the latest hats from Masons, whose rather elegant frontage can be seen on the left. Adjoining was Waltons Arcade; Waltons were a big name in Exeter right into the mid 1970s. Advertising for Kodak film occupies valuable space on the sun blinds of the chemists next door. Boots building, of course, together with its elegant facade, was sadly doomed. The loud voices of protest were ignored when the powers that be decided to build the new C&A stores, and the Victorian building at the corner of Queen Street and High Street fell prey to the hungry bulldozer. Thankfully, the Doric style of the Higher Market on the left (and surrounding buildings) was allowed to remain when the Guildhall Shopping Centre was built. The market, opened in 1838, became a focal point of city life, with thousands of people converging on Exeter every Friday. This would be the starting point for housewives around the city, who would tour the market to find the best - and cheapest - apples,

pears, oranges, grapefruit and bananas - all part of the traditional fun of bargain hunting.

Below: Sixpence to park your car all day seems a good enough offer, but in a road devoid of all traffic but a tram and a push bike, and where on-street parking was free and available, we have to wonder if the proprietors of the car park on the far left found running the facility worth their while! The picture dates from 1931. Note the marvellous old baby carriage on the left; mothers have come a long way since they had to push these huge prams around! The designers of old, however, had method in their madness; they built in a spacious storage space beneath the baby where you could put extra blankets, bottles, or your shopping! High above Cowick Street a train stands on St Thomas' station bridge, while Number 33 tramcar passes below. Note how close together the tramlines are in order to give the cars clearance under the bridge. The tracks remain separate, yet two trams are unable to pass each other. The layout saved the authorities having to install spring points at either side of the bridge. The first railway station at this spot opened in 1846 - just a wooden shed and a single platform at the time; it was named St Thomas' in 1897.

Exeter High Street has always had so much to offer; within the space of a few hundred yards you could get cash from a number of banks, shop for a new carpet for the lounge or lino for the kitchen, meet a friend for coffee or lunch, buy yourself a new leather handbag, choose a new pair of shoes - and catch a bus to get home in time for tea. The High Street might have changed, but although cars are today banned, perhaps more buses than ever use the High Street. A sharp eye might be able to pick out a bus approaching in the distance; we have no date for the photograph but trams no longer ran along High Street at the time - note the lack of tram lines. Exeter had electric trams for less than 30 years - the system was scrapped in 1931.

Right: It was around 1930 when a photographer set up his camera in Sidwell Street. The old trams were still running at the time - note the request stop mounted on the traction pole on the right. And how many readers remember those old signs: 'You may telephone from here'? Mobile phones lay far in the future.... Sidwell Street was devastated during World War II, though here and there among the bombed-out buildings were a very few that had been repaired, and the odd blocks that had escaped the bombs. The many shops and homes wiped out during the war were sadly missed; on the north side, the land between St Sidwell's Church and York Road, and on the south side between the site on which Homesense was built and the junction of Belmont Road and Blackboy Road, lay derelict. Always wide enough for cars to park down the middle, bombsites provided extra parking spaces in Sidwell Street for many years after the war - a sad benefit for motorists. Much of what was spared by the bombs, however, did not escape the red pen of the developers. Demolition and redevelopment of the area began in 1950 and continued until the mid 1960s, but the series of shops on the right survive today, as do the two older ones beyond them.

Below: In a view which pre-dates World War II, the flags fly over the portico of the Guildhall. We can only hazard a guess at what the occasion was; perhaps the flags were there to honour King George V's Silver Jubilee in 1935, or the coronation of his son George VI in 1937? Though the sun is shining, coats and hats are the order of the day among the people passing below the Guildhall's ancient portico, though one gentleman has made a concession to the weather, removing his coat to carry it over his arm. Hats, however, were a different matter. Before the mid 1940s few would have been seen out of doors without a hat or a cap, and the type of headgear worn by a man was a good indication of his station in life. While working men invariably opted for a flat cap, the managerial, middle-class gentleman would wear a smart bowler. Curry's cycles is a name which is still very familiar to us today; cycling enjoyed a huge following in Exeter, and we see from the signs in the window that you could acquire a cycle from two shillings a week. Was this to rent, or to buy, we wonder? This would probably be rental, we imagine; hire purchase was to become much more common during the late 1950s and 60s.

GETTING AWAY FROM IT ALL

By the end of the 1950s, many town centres which were unfortunate enough to lie along major city routes became bottlenecks, particularly on Bank Holidays. It was clear that something must be done to direct traffic away from town and city streets.

Britain's first stretch of motorway was not, as is popularly believed, the M1. The eight-and-a-quarter miles long Preston Bypass - later part of the M6 - was opened by Prime Minister Harold Macmillan in December 1958.

Vast swathes were cut through the outskirts of towns as ring roads were built to take traffic away from town centres. A network of motorways speeded the average journey, and by the end of the 20th century Britain had 2,015 miles of motorway.

Post-war prosperity meant that more families could aspire to that badge of one-upmanship - a new car. Hot off the production line in 1959 was the Mini - destined to become the 1960s 'car of the decade'.

Enemy bombing, coupled with the wholesale removal of some of Exeter's finest buildings, still brings a sense of sadness and outrage to those who remember the city as it used to be. This was Exeter High Street before the war, with the corner of Deller's Cafe on the far left of the shot; how many memories are stirred among those old enough to remember that marvellous place! The interior of Deller's was built to an unusual, tiered design, where diners ate in balconied splendour. Open every day between nine in the morning and nine in the evening, Deller's had a

whole range of different treats on offer, from the standard morning coffee and luncheon to their delicious Devonshire teas and fish suppers. The restaurant's ballroom and function rooms made special occasions such as retirement dinners, tea dances, Christmas balls and New Year parties even more special. With great optimism and unshakeable faith in the future, an advert in the 1936 Exeter Guide stated that 'Deller's will

always be Deller's' - a confidence that was sadly shattered during an enemy bombing raid on the night of 3rd May 1942, which left the opulent Deller's an empty shell. It could have been saved, but was not. Incidentally, Eland's (in the centre of the picture) is one of a handful of independent local traders still in existence today. The company specialise in maps and now occupy Mol's Coffee House.

Both pages: There was nothing you could do about it, so you might as well make the best of things - the looks of cheerful resignation on the faces of these flood victims rescued by lorry say it all *(below right)*! The day the River Exe burst its banks - 27th October 1960 - will be well remembered by readers unlucky enough to have had to cope with the ghastly mess. It wasn't just having to wade through three feet of water in your sitting room, trying to pile your precious furniture out of harm's way; it was the rest of it, the things people forget. It was being marooned in upstairs rooms; looking out for the cat, the dog or the rabbit; trying to keep the kids and grandma warm and dry and well fed. And when it was all over, surveying the hideous tidemarks on the wallpaper you hung only six months ago, and shedding tears over the state of your sodden Axminster.

There had been flooding in the past, but this was the worst that people had experienced in a lifetime. As the Exe burst free from its banks, a wave of water surged into Alphington Street, Haven Road, Cowick Street and Okehampton Street. People were taken aback by the frightening speed at which the floodwater flowed into their homes and shops. The Royal Oak, for example, was completely dry at 11.20, yet 40 minutes later it was six inches deep in water. The bridge, of course, was impassable, marooning people on either side and preventing them from getting to and from their homes. As the flood turned

the roads into rivers, a boat and a pair of oars was the only option for many - though submerged obstacles would have made progress rather hazardous *(right)*. Negotiating Cowick Street was tricky - and, if you wanted to keep your clothes dry, less than dignified. Passing traffic did not help those trying to go about their normal business; this passing lorry left a tidal wave in its wake that was enough to wet the highest hem and swamp the longest pair of wellies *(bottom)*. Help was at hand, though, for those who were worst hit. The Welfare Department stepped in and provided more than 100 meals for Exwick victims, and two rest centres were opened in case people needed to be evacuated. One couple, however, got themselves a unique souvenir to remind them of the occasion - a twelve-inch grayling which they discovered swimming around in their kitchen! They intended to have the unlucky fish stuffed and mounted; does it still exist, we wonder, swimming in perpetuity above a fireplace somewhere in Exeter?

High Street looked very different in the 1940s from that of today; wartime bombing coupled with modernisation and redevelopment put paid to many of these old buildings. Barratts, of course, still occupies the same position - but in what a different building! Sadly, the well-known footwear chain demolished this ancient, highly individual, twin-gabled structure after the second world war and replaced it with a typical 1950s angular building. Just out of shot in

the left foreground was Colsons, which was the place to shop for fashions in Exeter. How many readers remember the fashion shows they used to stage there? This building, too, was demolished and rebuilt; Dingles occupy the site today. The modern

Marks & Spencer now stands on the right, on the corner of Queen Street. As a sop to those who hated to see the old building go, the cupola on what was then Walton's was preserved and today tops the octagonal feature on the M&S building.

Left: *Cathedral Close has to be one of the most beautiful parts of Exeter. Under the shadow of the cathedral the Royal Clarence Hotel, as impressive today as it was when this photograph was taken in the 1950s, was opened as assembly rooms in the 18th century, and would have seen much gaiety at the regular balls held there. The proprietor of the establishment was a Frenchman, and he named it The Hotel - the first time the French word had been used in England. Many famous visitors have made the Royal Clarence their base when staying in Exeter, among them Lord Nelson himself; Queen Victoria's father, the Duke of Kent, was taken to the Royal Clarence when he died in 1820 in Sidmouth. The hotel owes its royal title to the Duchess of Clarence (later Queen Adelaide, wife of William IV), who made a point of lunching there and reputedly raved about the lobsters and the junket. Well, who wouldn't?*

Mol's Coffee House, on the right, dates from the late 16th century. It was run as a gentlemen's club and coffee house by an Italian by the name of Mol. Gentlemen of standing in the city would meet there to discuss the politics and business of the day, and read the news sheets which during the 18th century were commonly circulated around such clubs.

Below: *We can be very thankful that the Ship Inn, one of Exeter's most ancient hostelries, has survived to the present day. It has acquired a new sign, though, since this view along the very narrow St Martin's Lane was captured, probably some time in the 1940s. Ever a popular tourist city, many visitors would have been glad to take advantage of the 'Bed and Breakfast' that was being offered, considering it a real privilege to stay at the old inn, the favourite watering hole of Sir Francis Drake himself. The Elizabethan sea captain, who sailed around the world and brought back a shipload of Spanish treasure, was very partial to a pint or three at the Ship; in 1587 he wrote in a letter to a friend, 'Next to mine own shippe I do most love that old Shippe in Exon, a tavern in Fyssh Street' (an old name for St Martin's Lane). Drake was soon to face and beat the formidable Spanish Armada. The Ship Inn continued to crop up in historical records; during the Civil War some of Cromwell's soldiers were billeted here. The CO was well impressed - he wrote that the inn had 'good wine, victuals and forage, and an upright man for host'. What better testimony could be given?*

Above: A sight that will send many a reader on a trip down Memory Lane - the old ABC cinema in High Street. Many were the 'first dates' that took place within these well-remembered walls, and many were the cuddles on the back seat under the cover of darkness! 'Ryan's Daughter' was on the programme when this scene was snapped for posterity; a beautiful - if over long - film set in Ireland in the early years of the 20th century. Released in 1970, the film starred Robert Mitchum as a village schoolmaster and Sarah Miles as his young wife who falls for a handsome British officer - an age-old story which tugged at your heartstrings until you started looking at your watch....
A photographer standing in the same spot today would reveal a vastly different scene - though Boots' corner still carries its astrological clock. More mature readers will remember that during the 1930s and 40s the interval at the ABC - in those days the Savoy - was as entertaining as the films themselves. Who can forget those wonderful Harold Stringer concerts, which often went out on the radio? Those were the days! Exeter enjoyed the ABC for more than 50 years before it was demolished in September 1987 and replaced by shops.

Above right: Ideal school holiday viewing and how many of our readers remember queuing to see the magical 'Bedknobs and Broomsticks' in the far-off days of their childhood? Children loved the Walt Disney story of the three children and the good-natured witch who, with the aid of a flying bedstead, foiled the German plot to invade England. The critics, however, were not as kind when they compared the film to the superb 'Mary Poppins', calling it 'muddled' and 'incompetent'. Children too young to know the meaning of the word simply got on with enjoying the film....
It was the early 1970s when a photographer captured this

quiet scene. Few people were about to take notice, though a couple of impressive vehicles stand in Sidwell Street outside the Odeon. Opened in 1937, the 2,000 seat cinema was a model of the technology of the day, with the latest sound reproduction, earphones for the deaf, air conditioning and constantly-changing coloured lights. Cinemascope was fitted, of course, in the 1950s; readers may remember the protests when the group of life-sized medieval figures was removed during the alterations - and later returned by popular demand - only to be thrown out once again by the conversion of the cinema to three screen! We are fortunate that the Odeon managed to fight its way through the lean years when television put paid to many of our cinemas, and still survives to the present day.

Below: How many readers can confess to having tasted their first pint in the Turk's Head in Cowick Street? More than one, we would imagine. Exeter has had more than one 'Turk's Head', the more well known hotel of that name being situated in the High Street. The sign, however, was a popular one, and the history of the name itself can be traced back to the days of the Crusades.

When plans for the new shopping precinct were announced in the vicinity of this establishment they included a proposal to demolish the building along with many other adjacent properties. In 1972 the old Turk's Head was bulldozed to make way for the St Thomas' shopping precinct, the first in Exeter to be built with the car owner in mind. Its parking facilities for 100 cars did little to console those who were saddened by the removal of yet another piece of Exeter's irreplaceable history.

Bottom: Building and reconstruction went on apace during the 1950s, and the city we know today, built with modern materials, gradually emerged from the rubble. Exeter city centre had a new image; gone were many of its ancient architectural treasures, some involuntarily, others by design. Many hated the straight lines and characteristic vertical facades of the new buildings, but we learned to live with it, and the young men and women of today have known nothing else during their lifetime. This photograph dates from the early 1960s; by that time stores such as Kendalls, the rainwear manufacturer who 'keep you dry', Thomas Cook travel, Lennards footwear store and Marks and Spencer (still the favourite store of many Exeter shoppers in its present site at the Guildhall Centre) were up and running and enjoying a brisk trade on the day this photograph was taken. The view is notable for being pre-Debenhams. Then called Bobby's, it was built later in the 1960s, a 'high-rise' tower permitted because it was outside the city walls. Future years would see wider walkways, seats, trees and shrub tubs installed to soften the effect, and general traffic banned from the High Street - though buses were to remain.

The construction of a success set in concrete

The advent of the second world war signalled a period of change for the country and indeed, for the Exeter area itself. In fact, it was the declaration of war that initiated the foundation of the building firm, Exeter Building Contractors Limited as it was then known.

The war meant that many workers had to leave their jobs in order to join the armed forces and loyally serve their country. This left a shortage of workers and therefore, a need for larger companies that would be able to meet these workload demands. It was then, in this climate in 1939, that a group of builders in the Exeter area joined forces to form Exeter Building Contractors Limited, now called EBC Group plc. The two people largely responsible for the creation of the new business were, David Stoneman Senior and Frank Sleeman CBE, FCIOB.

David Stoneman Senior had built up considerable experience within the building industry before establishing Exeter Building Contractors Limited. When the first world war broke, David was still learning his trade serving his apprenticeship as a carpenter and joiner for E C Lea. However, because he was in the territorial army, he was sent straight to France at the declaration of war and had to put his apprenticeship on hold. David found himself bravely undertaking his duties in the trenches during the war and by 1918, he was serving as a "sapper" (Royal Engineer) for the 4th Devon's. It was not until he came out of the army that David was able to resume his apprenticeship. With his apprenticeship completed, David did not waste any time and by the early 1920s, after progressing to foreman, he harnessed his ambition and set up his own business building houses in Whipton.

By the year 1938, David Stoneman Senior had become a well established builder throughout the area. Indeed, it was in this same year that the Leader of the Building Federation arranged for him to meet with another successful local builder, Frank Sleeman. Frank Sleeman CBE was the son of Marwood Thomas

Above left: *Frank Sleeman, co-founder of the company.*
Below: *The Royal Clarence Hotel's extensive refurbishments which took place in the early 1990s.*

Sleeman, the founder of MT Sleeman, and indeed, he was involved in running the family firm when he met David Stoneman Senior. Frank had left his position at the Town Clerk's Office in 1910 in order to join his fathers' business which was, at the time, experiencing difficulties. However, by the time Frank had to leave to serve in the army in the first world war, the business was once again flourishing.

At the outbreak of world war two Frank's business lost contracts as workers joined up and materials became hard to get. Consequently, Frank wrote to the Ministry of Supply offering to co-ordinate local builders. It was through this offer that Frank met David. Upon meeting, the two men made the decision to jointly form a company which was initially intended to last

for the duration of the war. So, in 1939, Exeter Building Contractors Limited, later EBC and Sleeman Limited, and now EBC Group plc, was established.

The new business also included several other small building firms and amongst the other original directors were: Albert Adams; Frank Healy; and Frank Lea. The combined company was considered large enough to be able to meet the government criteria necessary to carry out second world war damage work, and this was the work the business first undertook. The company's first base was at Colleton Mews in Exeter and it was from there that

Above: *Reconstruction of Millets store, High Street, Exeter in 1980.*

EBC Limited took its first order. This was the task of making wooden ammunition boxes and they were, in fact, made by the hundred! This job was followed by work on Exeter Airport. The airport was considerably enlarged under tight security and this led to work on other defence installations. The company also combined forces with McAlpine to build a huge hutted camp at Lee Mill in Plymouth and many properties were converted into hospitals and convalescent homes. Then came the blitz...

The blitz threw the new firm into the thick of things and almost immediately its workload dramatically increased. Emergency repairs were carried out in Exeter, Plymouth, Bristol and London. Indeed, the day after Plymouth made its plea for help, 600 men were sent to the town on the train with each fare costing 1s 2½d - the equivalent of 6p return! As part of the emergency repairs, roof slates were improvised from linoleum and cellophane sheets became windows! With the city in flames it was hot work for the people on fire watch duty, extinguishing fire bombs and small blazes before they had chance to take hold. The new company received official approval from the Ministry of Works

> *Exeter suffered from bombing raids during the war - EBC carrying out a magnitude of repairs*

and as a result were allocated more and more jobs. After the V1 and V2 flying bombs began to rain down, hundreds of workers went to London. Frighteningly, the company's employees experienced many 'close calls' as these dreadful weapons landed nearby to their sites. Exeter itself suffered heavily from German bombing and its centre had been largely swept away. As a result, EBC Limited carried out a considerable magnitude of repairs but fortunately, and rather miraculously, the Cathedral and its surrounding buildings around the green and the Guildhall area remained standing despite being quite badly damaged.

By the cessation of hostilities, because of the extent of its work, the newly formed company had become highly organised. Indeed, because it had become so well established, Frank and David made the decision not to disband their company as planned, but to continue trading after the war as a contracting entity, carrying out building and engineering work. The firm continued in business and EBC Group was born.

Top: *Work underway on Winslade Manor new offices with the old manor in the background under protective cover.*

Having played an important part in the war effort, the firm also had much to do with post-war reconstruction in Exeter. Work was carried out in the laying of new roads and the construction of deep sewers in the central area such as, High Street, Bedford Street, Paris Street and Summerland Street. A number of new stores and offices were also erected in the locality of Princesshay and the High Street. Other work included: several buildings at Exeter University; countless houses throughout the city. Indeed, the decade came to a successful end for the company and especially for Frank Sleeman, as in 1948 he was given the honour of being made the National President of the Federation of Building Trade Employers.

Throughout the 1950s the company continued with its reconstruction work. Bomb craters and red sandstone were tunnelled through to create new sewers, often producing the comic effect of tunnel gangs emerging with very red faces! Labour and equipment was in short supply during these years and as a result, old War Department concrete mixers and water pumps were called into service. To compensate for the labour shortage, the company even borrowed a gang of 20 prisoners and two wardens from Exeter Prison. The prisoners helped out with work in New Bedford Street every day and worked very hard in order to keep their 'jobs' in the fresh air!

In 1954, the flourishing company experienced further expansion and development. It was in this year that David persuaded Frank not to retire but to stay on in the company under the new name of EBC and Sleeman Limited, which reflected the merger between Exeter Building Contractors Limited and MT Sleeman and Sons Limited. The latter firm had been established in 1897 by Frank Sleeman's father, Marwood T Sleeman, and had carried out many large contracts in the South Western counties. However, less than a year later, David Stoneman Senior died and sadly, the productive partnership came to an end. But, as his name suggests, David left a son, David Stoneman, who had worked for the firm during his summer holidays from school and university. He officially joined the company in 1952 as Site Agent and was later to carry on the family name within the business by becoming Chairman of EBC in 1969.

The newly merged firm continued to thrive. It extended its activities further by becoming owners of E A Mitchelmore and Sons Limited and John Davey and Son Limited, both of which traded as building contractors in Torquay and South Devon respectively, and also by becoming associated with the Exeter firm of A J Adams Limited. EBC was in an extremely healthy position when, in the early 1960s, the second of its founder members, Frank Sleeman CBE, eventually decided to retire from the day-to-day administration of the firm. This year was also an important one for another of the company's long-serving members of staff, J C Deem. Mr Deem joined MT Sleeman and Sons in the early 1930s and in 1960 was awarded the British Empire Medal for his work as a general foreman in the building industry.

By 1961, the company had expanded to such an extent that it was necessary to move from Colleton Mews in

Above left: *David Stoneman, son of the co-founder, David Stoneman senior.* ***Below:*** *New hospitality suites built at Newton Abbot Racecourse.*

Melbourne Street, which had been the company's base for over 20 years. The offices, stores and yard at the base had to be demolished to provide for development by Exeter City Council, so EBC moved to new headquarters at Marwood House, 60 St David's Hill in Exeter. The new headquarters provided larger and more up-to-date offices and the company also erected a new garage, stores and plant depot on another site at Harrington Lane, Pinhoe. Further work carried out during this period included the rebuilding of Colsons in six stages and the extension of the Guildhall.

This decade also saw the emergence of John Garnsworthy who had taken over the role as Managing Director in 1959. Originally a trainee estimator with the Group, John had joined the company straight from school at the age of 16! By the end of 1963, Frank Sleeman had persuaded him to accept the position of Chairman. Indeed, in his later years Frank Sleeman had marked down John Garnsworthy and David Stoneman as people of considerable potential and had groomed them for the future. This choice proved to be a wise one as, with the considerable energy and imagination of David and John behind it, EBC expanded its activities to become a regional contracting company operating throughout the South West. The company widened its activities to cover: Plant Hire (Beacon Plant Limited); Plastering (Andrew Brothers Limited); Mechanical and Electrical (Hodgson Heating Limited); Joinery (Chancel Joinery Limited); Shopfitting (Heppel Chancel Limited); Roofing (ABC Roofing Limited); Scaffolding (Gardners Scaffolding Limited); and with considerable input from Les Wint, EBC Developments was also formed.

During the 20 years leading up to the 1980s EBC Group enjoyed a period of sustained growth. The company expanded its activities into Cornwall and opened contracting offices in Bristol and Bournemouth. It also continued to carry out construction activities under the name of Sleeman Construction, and building and maintenance activities under the names of: M T Sleeman; Cruse and Bridgeman; Hill and Lang; Wilkins and Coventry; and Rutland Builders. In this period, EBC Group carried out many prestigious schemes including: the Main Ward blocks at Torbay Hospital; C&A and Dingles in Exeter; the Byron Hotel in London; Broadwalk House and Northernhay House in Exeter; and over 400 houses plus the swimming pool and hospital in Weymouth. Several of these contracts would individually, in today's terms, have exceeded £15 million. Indeed, the company was awarded

Above: *Walnut House, group headquarters from the early 1970s to 1990.* ***Below:*** *Broadwalk House, Exeter, built by the company in the early 1970s.*

the most valuable job in the Exeter area when they won the contract at Wyvern Barracks, followed by the tallest job in the area when they won the contract for the 10-storey block at Exeter College. With the onset of the cold war, the company was also involved in re-providing defence installations which had previously been 'stood down'. The firm's employees had to endure uncomfortable rides in the back of a lorry on Monday mornings in order to undertake work at airfields and radar stations around the coasts. New water supplies, reservoirs, sewers and sewage works also had to be tackled which meant the development of new skills and the development of special tools and equipment. Several landmarks on the hills around the city date from this activity including, Blackhill, Dunsford and Perridge.

This period, without the dangers of a world war, nonetheless had its own perils. Indeed, there were a few disasters along the way, including the collapse of an historic wall behind the High Street and the fall of a large shop into a basement under construction in Taunton! One frantic night, the top floors of the main building of the R D & E Hospital caught fire and burnt out. In the evacuation, EBC was on site by eight in the morning organising a massive scaffold framework and roofing to enable the rebuilding to proceed day and night. A nasty accident was also narrowly avoided when on another job, a ½ ton bucket of cement caught on scaffolding and fell 80 feet, landing between the foreman and the supervisor!

During the second half of the 1970s, EBC Group carried out several major projects. Amongst them was the construction of the Poole Arts Centre which commenced in 1975 and was completed in 1978. The Centre contained a 1300 seater main auditorium, a 500 seater theatre, an art gallery, exhibition areas, the HQ building of the Western Orchestral Society and ancillary restaurants, bars and public areas. At the time of construction the building was the most advanced of its kind in Europe and is still regarded as one of the most acoustically advanced buildings of its kind. Another significant project during these years was at Winslade Manor. Under the Contracts Manager, Richard Boutle (now Regional Managing Director of EBC Construction), offices at the Manor were built by EBC to house the 500 staff of London and Manchester Assurance, who were relocated from their

Above left: EBC Group's first non-executive directors appointed in 1985. Nick Williams (left) and Brian Jennings. ***Top:*** *The EBC board circa 1987. Standing left to right: Peter Evans, Les Wint, Ian Baker, Nick Williams, Sam Clark, Brian Jennings. Seated left to right: Tony Hopper, Bert Cockroft, David Stoneman, John Garnsworthy, Cyril Turner.*

London offices. The existing manor house was fully refurbished as executive Headquarters and the existing blocks were converted and extended to form a Leisure complex for the staff. Despite some 200 people working on the project, the rumoured underground tunnel between the existing Manor House and Bishop's Court Palace was never found! The success of the project was rewarded when the contractor won several awards for the project including: a Civic Trust Award; a Royal Institute of British Architects' Award; and a Concrete Society Award. Indeed, the success of the company as a whole was highlighted during this time when, in 1977, it was David Stoneman who was given the important role of meeting the Prime Minister, James Callaghan, to discuss possible measures to improve the position of the construction industry.

By 1981, EBC Group had successfully flourished to such an extent that it was able to become a public company and seven years later in 1988, this status progressed to a full Stock Exchange listing. In 1982,

the current Chief Executive, Peter Evans, was appointed to the EBC Group Board where he worked alongside David Stoneman, John Garnsworthy, Cyril Turner, John Andrews, Ian Baker, and Les Wint. During the 1980s the Group achieved considerable growth but also recognised the need to relieve itself of some of its non-core activities. It was also at around this time, in 1986, that for the first time, two Non-Executive Directors, Nick Williams and Brian Jennings, joined the Group Board bringing

Left: John Garnsworthy - former chairman and managing director of EBC. Below: The main auditorium of Poole Arts Centre, Bournemouth which was built between 1975-78. Bottom: Longbrook House, new offices for the Inland Revenue at New North Road, Exeter built in 1993.

invaluable experience to the company. In the same year Bert Cockroft joined the EBC Group as Chief Executive. Initially, Bert's role was to create a line of succession for David Stoneman and John Garnsworthy, but his main early tasks also included the rationalisation of EBC and the divestment of a number of the non-core activities. Bert achieved this difficult task within a fairly short timetable and eventually succeeded David Stoneman as Chairman at the end of 1990, whilst retaining the role of Chief Executive. In his retirement speech, David Stoneman commented on the successful progression of the company, which had reached its Golden Jubilee year. He also expressed his confidence that the next fifty years would be just as successful.

Peter Evans joined EBC Group in 1969 as a Quantity Surveyor. From 1981 to 1992 he ran the construction side of EBC, before becoming Deputy Chief Executive. At the end of 1995, he succeeded Bert Cockroft as Chief Executive with the Group Board including; Non-Executive Chairman, Bob Carlton-Porter and Non-Executive Director, Louis Sherwood. The rest of the Board, still in tact today, comprised; Tony Davies (Construction); Ian Franklin (Developments); Mike Bailey (Financial Director); Barry Smith; and Julian Turnbull as Group

Company Secretary. At the beginning of 1997, the Group continued its success and as a result, was able to acquire Spaceage Plastics Limited, a builders' merchant specialising in the sale of plastic building materials and the specialist manufacture of conservatory roofs. A year later, in 1998, the Group acquired NR Humphreys (Contracts) Limited, a building and maintenance company based in Reading and in doing so, gave further geographical spread to the Group's building and maintenance activities.

Today, EBC Group continues to build upon its outstanding reputation, first secured by David Stoneman Senior and Frank Sleeman CBE, FCIOB, all that time ago, in 1939. From its foundation as a temporary arrangement, EBC Group has certainly come along way, firmly constructing a success set in concrete which will, no doubt, last for many more years to come!

Above centre: One of many EBC sponsorships of young people, this one in support of young expeditioners.
Top: The opening of Mountbatten Water Sports' Centre, Plymouth by the Duke of Edinburgh. The people on the left of the photograph are (from left to right): Ray Jude (Contracts Manager), Eddie Binding (Site Agent), Bill Bond (Labourer), Peter Evans (Chief Executive).

A grand day out

It was 13th August 1907 when this group of day-trippers posed proudly for this photograph - the little ones no doubt told to stand still and 'watch the birdie'. No birdie was forthcoming, of course, to the disappointment of many a child, but the ploy usually did the trick in making them look at the camera! The fact that the group was pictured outside Oliver's boot and shoe shop in the High Street could have special significance. Perhaps this was an outing arranged for staff and their families? Be that as it may, in spite of the solemn looks, the children, buckets and spades at the ready, are obviously looking forward to a day by the sea. Oliver's, whose marvellous lanterns in the background inform passers-by that they are the 'largest retailer of shoes in the world', are still going strong in Exeter High Street, today as Oliver & Timpson. To the right of the photograph is F. W. Salisbury's, whose 'leather goods, trunks and portmanteaux' were to bring them fame; the firm still survives, though a couple of doors away on the opposite side of the shoe shop.

Everyone loves a day out, especially if the sun shines. The weather looked reasonably good for this particular party, though these happy trippers are taking no chances, and are wearing their coats and hats just in case. The occasional day trip was a welcome break from the daily routine, whether your day was spent in the office or at the kitchen sink, and once the charabanc was bowling along at an impressive 12mph, the sun and wind would blow any workaday blues away. We can only hope that the ladies' hats were safe!

The vehicle was convertible, and in the event of rain the fold-down hood would be hastily fixed in place.

Many of the 'charas' served a dual purpose; during the week they acted as delivery vehicles, then when the weekend came, rows of seats were added ready for those trips to the seaside that became popular with office and shop workers during the 1920s and 30s. The trips offered a great day out at a reasonable price, and all the family could go along; the charas lacked luggage space, however, and one toddler's push chair has been tied to the lamp.

Left: How nice it is, just once in a while, to do nothing and then rest afterwards! When the coach reached its destination - wherever that was - the beach would beckon, and the mothers and grandmothers on this church trip would no doubt hire a deck chair and take a well-earned rest. Things were different, however, for the children. For them, there was plenty to do - and sitting in deck chairs was not one of them! They had done enough sitting in the coach. With buckets and spades at the ready they would make a beeline for the sands, where they could get stuck into building castles and digging moats which would fill with water as the tide came in. Funfairs, shops, putting greens and even the formal rose gardens all presented a welcome change from the realities of working life.

Above: The distinctive wrought iron holder which holds up the oil lamp in this picture can still be seen at the time of writing. The delicately fashioned structure stands outside Holy Trinity Parish Hall and Sunday School, not far from the site of the old South Gate. The bishop laid the foundation stone for the Parish Hall in September 1913. In more recent times the building became the New Theatre of the Cygnet Theatre Training School, and Holy Trinity Church itself went on to be the location of the White Ensign Club for retired and active members of the Royal Navy and Royal Marines. Back to the picture, and we notice a number of children aboard the bus seemingly fretting at the delay caused by the taking of photographs. These little chaps will be senior citizens today - fathers and grandfathers themselves.

It was a butcher, Sam Sluggett, who became Exeter's first charabanc operator. He acquired his 22-seat Leyland vehicle after the Great War and launched into the day trip business.

Above: Life's a game - but rugby, as we all know, is serious stuff! It was April 1907 when this 12,000 strong, all-male crowd of rugby fans turned out to watch Devon play Durham in the Rugby County Championship final. The game ended without score and with their 0-0 draw the teams shared the title. Two years earlier the County ground had been the scene of a spectacular and unexpected thrashing when the New Zealand All Blacks played Devon in their very first match in Britain. Their innovatory play left crowd and players alike stunned - the New Zealanders won 55-4. There was no bad feeling, however, and the visitors were hailed as heroes.

Even in the early 20th century sports grounds were almost as popular with advertisers as they are today. 'Tighe's Ammonine' obviously died a death over the years - probably due to the fact that colds and influenza were not cured by it after all. The beef extract Bovril, however, stayed the course and remains a household name. Lovers of trivia might like to know that the catchphrase 'Bovril prevents that sinking feeling' was designed before World War I but was withheld at the time as a mark of respect for the families of those lost on the 'Titanic'.

Above right: In a scene reminiscent of Jerome's 'Three Men in a Boat', light slacks and straw boaters are the preferred 'cool' outfits among these dapper young men, pictured on a day out on the Exeter Canal during the early years of the 20th century. Amazing, isn't it, how little the Double Locks public house has changed?

Exeter has been using and enjoying the canal for hundreds of years; begun in 1566, it brought in goods such as sugar, wine and timber, and carried away vessels bearing textiles to sell overseas. As recently as the late 1930s around 50,000 tons of traffic used the Exeter Ship Canal; today, most of the commercial trade has disappeared from the canal and from the quayside. Pleasure boats and river and canal trips have replaced the old barges, and tourists wander where seagoing vessels once loaded up with their various cargoes. As rail and road links improved, the industrial life of the area started on a gradual decline which was halted by a forward-looking attitude towards the leisure industry. With its nature reserve, angling, souvenir and craft shops, fine visitor centre and summertime jazz concerts, the river and canal are today enjoying a new lease of life.

A day on the river - and with no chance of a ducking! We are given no date for this photograph, but this was almost certainly the big freeze of 1917, when the Exe froze so hard it was almost solid. The ice was thick enough to support the weight of around a hundred people who even if they couldn't skate were out to have fun. Thick coats, fur collars, warm scarves and mittens were the order of the day; note the lady wearing a muff. These fashion accessories were made of warm fur and hung around the neck; the ladies' hands were pushed inside to keep warm. Quite picturesque - but not so handy as a nice pair of sheepskin gloves! Closer examination reveals that the baby, snug and warm in his or her baby carriage, is wide awake and seems to be taking everything in; he has not been trusted to the ice, however! But what a marvellous piece of elegant engineering is that perambulator! The Exe has frozen over from time to time, but because of the moderate climate this has been a very rare occurrence and has not happened in recent years. The greenhouse effect perhaps?

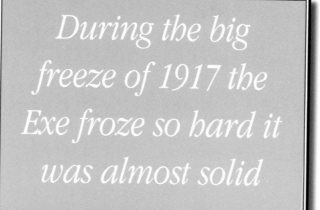

During the big freeze of 1917 the Exe froze so hard it was almost solid

to all parts.

'Parties conveyed to all parts' declares the sign on top of this vehicle. But with around 25 passengers to be crammed into a coach the size of a modern mini-bus, surely one coach is far too small for such a large party? We can not be certain, either, what kind of horse power the vehicle used - the motorised kind, or the four-legged sort! Certainly, a private hire service operated in Exeter in 1912, run by two brothers, William and Gilbert Greenslade. Their vehicle was a Model T Ford tourer fitted with a horse brake body. The later tour operators used the charabancs which rapidly gained popularity

Tour operators used charabancs, which gained popularity in the early years of the 20th century

in the early years of the 20th century. But wherever - and however - this group were heading they would have been looking forward to having a good time. After all, a day out is a day out, whatever your station in life. The smart clothes of these people proclaim them as being from the middle class; businessmen and their wives and children on a privately-arranged trip, perhaps. We will never know.

Left: Look closely at this picture - all is not what it seems at first glance! The wardrobes of brothers, husbands and fathers have obviously been raided to provide party costumes for this group of adventurous young ladies from Pearce's draper's store. We understand that these were all buyers for the firm. Whatever the occasion, they were out for a good time, and hats and ties, trousers and jackets - and a few moustaches - achieved the desired rakish look - though one girl has opted for the top hat and tails effect, complete with bow tie. The shoes, though, give the game away. There was no way the girls could turn Fred or Bill's size eleven canal barges into a dainty size five, so the footwear had to be their own. The cigarettes dangling from their mouths add a rather daring touch; this was the 1930s, and ladies who smoked out of doors were definitely frowned upon and regarded as rather 'fast'. It was OK, though, if you were a bloke - so that made everything all right for the Pearce's party!

Below: Staff trips are a thing of the past today, but for many years the annual outing was an event eagerly looked forward to by every large (and sometimes small) firm's workforce. The staff trip remained a long held tradition in the 1950s, but within the next twenty years or so rising costs meant that the writing was on the wall for the custom, and it began to die out. The happy crowd pictured here is the workforce of Willeys engineering, at one time Exeter's biggest employer. The tradition of staff trips goes back at least a hundred years, and possibly much longer than that. With some firms the custom began as a reward to workers after they had worked particularly hard to meet a client's deadline, putting in extra hours in the evenings and at weekends. The firm would hire horse-powered transport or a charabanc and the entire staff was driven out into the countryside or to the seaside, where games and races would often be arranged and tea would be taken at a local inn or tearoom. With the advent of railways, of course, the choice of destination expanded considerably.

Both pictures: We can almost feel the suppressed excitement among these children, whose huge grins of genuine delight say it all *(bottom)*. The knapsacks and carrier bags of food give us a hint; this is the day of the school trip - the day the children have been looking forward to for many weeks. Are the staff feeling the same, we wonder? The half a dozen adults look cheerful enough as they group up for the routine photograph; will they feel the same way when the 80 or so pupils board their coaches or their train and head off to the seaside, we wonder? The annual school trip is not the most relaxing time for the teaching staff! A second group of children, pictured on the railway platform are also definitely travelling by train *(right)*. The year is 1951, and the destination is Paignton. The packs of sandwiches, clutched tightly by all the children, are probably intended for consumption on the beach; we must hope that they did not end up acting as missiles in a dispute between the boys and the girls! But then, children seemed rather better behaved back then. In the 1950s, some schoolteachers still reinforced strict discipline and the learning of the 'three Rs' by the application of a cane across the palm. Not a pleasant memory for those who remember the painful tingling that could last for up to an hour afterwards!

Sporting life

This page and overleaf: St James's Park was merely a farmer's field when the first Exeter soccer club shared its facilities with rugby players, a herd of cows and the odd

travelling circus (though not simultaneously!) back in the late 19th century.

It was a rather sparse crowd of fans who turned out to watch Exeter face Bristol *(above)*, and judging by the rather bored expression on the face of the young lad leaning on the boundary fence, not too much was happening on the pitch when the photographer happened by with his camera. The well-dressed tot in lacy cap, light coat and shiny boots perched on top appears to be enjoying herself, however, and with her proud Dad's arm to support her she knows she is in little danger of falling off. It is interesting to note that just about every one in this particular group of spectators appears to be well-to-do. Each wears his or her preferred form of headgear, from schoolboy's cap to bowler hat; the elaborate hat of the lady standing behind is a joy to behold (and probably needed perfect posture to balance it well!).

A lot of water has passed under the bridge since Exeter played their first match against West Ham United on 14th October 1911, and though City's fortunes have fluctuated over the years, the club has much to be proud of - and strangely enough that includes their defeats as well as their victories. Their praiseworthy sporting attitude, for example, when they walked the victorious Sunderland team to St David's Station to see them off on their journey home in the early 30s, is well worth a mention.

A QUESTION OF SPORT

Manchester United FC were left reeling when an air crash claimed the lives of seven of the 'Busby Babes' and left Matt Busby in a critical condition on 6th February 1958. The plane carrying the team crashed on takeoff from Munich.

The year 1964 saw American boxer Cassius Clay - later Muhammad Ali (I float like a butterfly, sting like a bee') - beat Sonny Liston to become world champion. In later life he developed Parkinson's disease, but saw himself voted Sportsman of the Century as the new Millennium began.

Wembley Stadium saw scenes of jubilation when on 30th July 1966 England beat West Germany 4-2 in the World Cup. It was Geoff Hurst's two dramatic goals scored in extra time that secured the victory and lifted the cup for England - at last.

The four-minute mile that had remained the record since 1945 was smashed on 6th May 1954 by Oxford University student Roger Bannister. He accomplished the seemingly impossible in three minutes 59.4 seconds, collapsing at the end of his last amazing lap.

Even football teams need relaxation from time to time, and this carefully-posed shot of the players about to leave St James's Park on the club's annual outing was taken, as far as we can gather, in 1929 *(below, main picture)*. With the players in the leading coach and the management and directors following on, everyone looks remarkably prim, well-behaved and with their Sunday best on. No photographs were taken of the lads at the end of the day....

The 1930-31 season went down in the records as City's glory days of the Cup Run (echoed in 1981), which began with a 3-0 win at Northfleet United and continued with a 2-1 score over Coventry City. Around 16,500

supporters crowded into St James's Park to watch their team play the mighty Derby County - and win 3-2. They reached the sixth round, but bitter disappointment followed when they were beaten by Sunderland. Keeping fit was as much as priority in the 1930s as it is today, and framed against the background of the old 'cowshed' standing terrace, we can see that skipping was no child's play to the team *(below inset)*. On the far right, nearest the camera, is Ernie Hobbs, who during his one season with Exeter played 11 times for City.

Fixtures against Clapton Orient (which after the second world war became Leyton Orient) figured regularly on the programme, and in a match that saw some exciting action, Orient's keeper W Robertson makes a desperate bid to keep City from scoring *(previous page, bottom picture)*. In spite of their recent successes, the 30s were difficult years for Exeter. In 1936 the club had to apply for re-election for the second time and manager Jack English signed around 60 new players in his search to give the club an infusion of new blood.

Events & occasions

Both pictures: Drawn by the drama and the tragedy, great crowds of people congregated on Exe Bridge when a runaway tram came to grief on 7th March 1917. The incident had actually begun some minutes before when the tram car number 12 came to a sudden stop half way up Paris Street. The driver, a Mr Sanders, managed to get the car re-started, and all went as normal - until it reached Fore Street. It was a terrifying moment for Mr Sanders when he realised that his brakes had failed; in spite of all his efforts to keep control the tram took off, swiftly gaining speed as it ran down Fore Street's one in eleven-and-a-half gradient. The first casualty was a railway contractor's horse and dray which was unfortunate enough to be pulling out to pass a parked barrow just as the runaway tram reached it. The horse, sadly, did not survive...but worse was to come. The five terrified passengers and the conductress could only hold on in terror as the tram rocketed on down the hill. As it reached the bridge the car left the rails, sped on, rocking and swaying, for a few yards, then crashed on to its right side, scattering splintered woodwork and broken glass across the road. The conductress, though badly cut and suffering from shock, was able to walk from the wreckage. Others, however, were not so lucky. Mrs Mary Findlay was killed outright, and the driver and two of his passengers were admitted to hospital. The chairman of the Tramways Committee and other officials were quickly on the scene to offer their help and take stock of the damage. The badly damaged tram was eventually hauled off to the shed, where it remained for a number of years. It was judged to be too costly for repair, and was scrapped in 1921.

ROYAL WATCH

The talking point of the early 1930s was the affair of the Prince of Wales, later King Edward VIII, and American divorcee Wallis Simpson. Faced with a choice, Edward gave up his throne to marry her. His Nazi sympathies were kept strictly under wraps at the time.

By the end of World War II, the 19-year-old Princess Elizabeth and Lieutenant Philip Mountbatten RN were already in love. The couple's wedding on 20th November 1947 was a glittering occasion - the first royal pageantry since before the war.

King George VI's health had been causing problems since 1948, when he developed thrombosis. In 1951 the King - always a heavy smoker - became ill again, and he was found to be suffering from lung cancer. He died in the early hours of 6th February 1952.

Princess Margaret's announcement in 1960 that she was to wed photographer Antony Armstrong-Jones brought pleasure to many who had sympathised when she ended her relationship with Peter Townsend in 1955. Her marriage to Lord Snowdon itself ended in 1978.

It was a red-letter day for the city when Exeter erected a statue of the much admired and respected General Redvers Buller on 6th September 1905. Thousands of people turned out to watch as the procession of important guests, civic dignitaries and representatives of the services made their way towards Bury Meadow, where an immense crowd had assembled to watch the unveiling ceremony. The Lord Lieutenant of Devon,

the third Earl Fortescue, did the honours and unveiled the statue, which depicted the famous general astride his horse. You cannot, of course, please all the people all the time, and a few voices were raised in protest when they discovered that General Buller faced away from his home town, Crediton. However, the four-and-a-half ton statue understandably stayed put, and Exeter simply got used to it. General Buller was awarded the Victoria Cross during the South African War of 1878-79, and broke the siege of Ladysmith in 1900, which is why the plinth bears the inscription 'He Saved Natal'. The General was still alive at the time of the unveiling and himself attended.

Left: Pictured on 9th January 1937, the smiling faces of Exeter St Thomas Salvation Army band, with their bandmaster Mr R Northwood and commanding officers Captain and Mrs Page. The Salvation Army, ridiculed and even physically attacked in the early days of their existence, quickly gained respect, not only in Exeter but across the country. Their high standards and reputation for good deeds gave the organisation a real standing in the community. How often have we, as children, followed the Salvation Army's processions and listened to the rousing music of the band? The Army owes its existence to William Booth, a young man with a deep concern for suffering of the poorest members of society. He trained as a Methodist minister, but later became dissatisfied with the lack of concern for the needs of the poor, and resigned. He preached in tent meetings and dance halls, urging his hearers, rich and poor alike, to turn to Christ for salvation. For Booth and his followers, the war against indifference and poverty was a very real one, and in 1878, along with

their military-style uniform, the Salvationists adopted the name that was to become famous around the world.

Below: 'Oh, mister porter, whatever shall I do? I want to go to Paddington, they've landed me at Crewe....' The old song could well have been part of this ingenious sketch put on by the children of Newtown Primary School. Music and song was the main element of the day - this was the school's entry for the 1949 Schools Music Festival. Newtown Primary's offering obviously had a railway theme, and their entry was worked out down to the smallest detail. Here are the passengers, the caterers with their refreshments trolley complete with cups and saucers, the porter, wearing appropriate overalls, with his trolley and suitcase - and the uniformed station master, ready to blow the whistle and see the train on its way. The clever entry deserved to win the first prize - perhaps some of our readers will recognise themselves as one of these enthusiastic youngsters, and will remember the occasion.

MILESTONES ALONG THE WAY

On 29th May 1953
Sir Edmund Hillary and Sherpa Tenzing Norgay conquered Everest, the world's highest mountain, using the most modern equipment of the day. On the summit they left the Union Jack, the flag of Nepal and the United Nations flag.

During the 1950s a lethal *mix of smoke and fog - labelled smog - descended regularly on Britain's town's and cities. In London alone the deaths of over 4,000 people were directly linked to smog in 1952. Three years later the Clean Air Act was passed to address the problem.*

Twenty-eight year old *Ruth Ellis went to the gallows in July 1955 for murdering her former lover, racing driver David Blakely. She was the last of 15 women hanged for murder in Britain during the 20th century. Capital Punishment ended in 1964.*

Decimalisation brought *confusion (and a rise in prices) to Britain in 1968. It was far easier to reckon in tens than in twelves and twenties, but all the same it was to be years before people stopped checking prices by mentally converting them into 'old money'.*

This picture and following pages: Everyone loves a parade - especially if there is a band to keep everyone in step, and people came out en masse to view this one, forming a tightly-packed crowd along the route. Possibly taken in 1936, we have no date for this group of photographs taken in Sidwell Street. However, as King George V died on 20th January that year, and the

COAL
OFFICE

Prince of Wales was proclaimed Edward VIII, one might be forgiven for thinking that this could have been the proclamation procession held in Exeter on 22nd January. Around that time there was genuine sadness, of course, at the death of the popular monarch, but the proclamation of a new one called for the flags and Union Jacks to be taken out of storage and strung across the streets. The scenes on the streets of Exeter would have been very similar to those depicted here, but the lack of characteristic mourning displays leads our 'picture detectives' to believe otherwise....

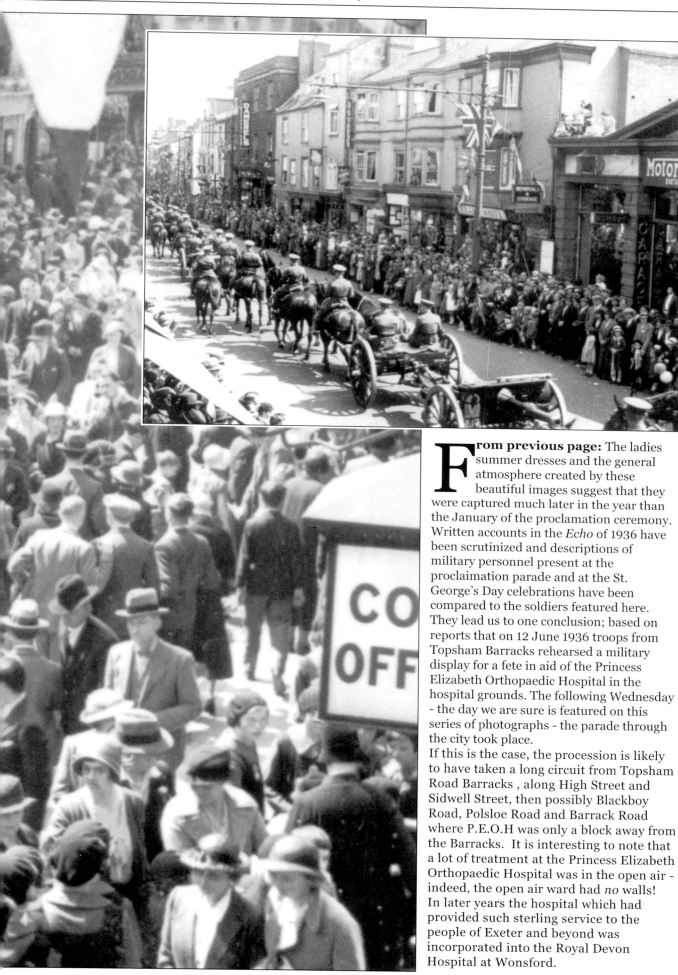

From previous page: The ladies summer dresses and the general atmosphere created by these beautiful images suggest that they were captured much later in the year than the January of the proclamation ceremony. Written accounts in the *Echo* of 1936 have been scrutinized and descriptions of military personnel present at the proclaimation parade and at the St. George's Day celebrations have been compared to the soldiers featured here. They lead us to one conclusion; based on reports that on 12 June 1936 troops from Topsham Barracks rehearsed a military display for a fete in aid of the Princess Elizabeth Orthopaedic Hospital in the hospital grounds. The following Wednesday - the day we are sure is featured on this series of photographs - the parade through the city took place.

If this is the case, the procession is likely to have taken a long circuit from Topsham Road Barracks , along High Street and Sidwell Street, then possibly Blackboy Road, Polsloe Road and Barrack Road where P.E.O.H was only a block away from the Barracks. It is interesting to note that a lot of treatment at the Princess Elizabeth Orthopaedic Hospital was in the open air - indeed, the open air ward had *no* walls! In later years the hospital which had provided such sterling service to the people of Exeter and beyond was incorporated into the Royal Devon Hospital at Wonsford.

FURTHER AFIELD....

Plans to develop the economies of member states into one common market came into being on 1st January 1958, when the EEC was formed. The original members were France, Belgium, Luxembourg, The Netherlands, Italy, and West Germany. Britain became a member in 1973.

Barbed wire and concrete blocks divided East from West when the infamous wall was built across the city of Berlin in 1961. Many escaped to the West at the eleventh hour, taking with them what they could carry. The Berlin Wall divided the city until 1989, when Communist rule collapsed.

The 2nd March 1969 was a landmark in aviation history. The Anglo-French supersonic airliner Concorde took off for the first time from Toulouse in France. Concorde was designed to fly from London to New York in an incredible three hours twenty minutes.

Neil Armstrong made history as the first man to set foot on the moon on 20th July 1969, and the phrase 'One giant leap for mankind' was coined. Twenty-one hours and thirty-seven minutes after their landing, he and 'Buzz' Aldrin took off again, proudly leaving the American flag on the Moon's surface.

Both pictures: The coronation of King George VI was a day that the people of Exeter celebrated in style. Not only were there the official events to look forward to, but there were the many street parties, dances and fireworks parties to enjoy. The coronation celebrations, held on 12th May 1937, did not go according to the original plan, however. On the death of George V, Britain had expected the Prince of Wales to take the throne and go on to reign for many years. Edward VIII, however, was King for

less than a year before he renounced the throne so that he could marry the American divorcee Wallis Simpson, hurling his younger brother Albert, Duke of York, unexpectedly into the kingship he had not been trained for. The following summer the coronation - and the parties - went ahead anyway, and as long as the jellies and cakes were on offer, few of these children enjoying their party at

Union Street school would have cared which king was on the throne! Each child was given a brand new coronation mug, most of which would have been carried carefully home and given pride of place on the mantelpiece - at least, until the novelty of the new king's reign wore off. How many of these mugs still survive, we wonder, tucked away in display cabinets or on delf racks around the city?

Above: King George and Queen Elizabeth with their two beautiful daughters endeared themselves to the bomb-weary people of Britain when they lived and suffered with the people through the dark days of war. They made a point of visiting towns and cities which had suffered heavy air raids - and Exeter, of course, was high on the agenda after the devastating blitz of 1942. The King and Queen, visiting on 8th May 1942, could not take away the heartache of so much great loss (1,500 homes totally destroyed and almost twice that number badly damaged; Dellers Cafe, the new library, the hospital as well as many shops, pubs, churches and banks), but at least they showed they cared. They toured the city, hearing many stories of the bravery of the city's unsung heroes - and Exeter wore a smile that day. The King and Queen (seen here in Clifton Street) showed great courage by staying on in England when they could have been evacuated to safety. They insisted that they be treated like everyone else, even to wartime rationing, and the King was almost relieved when Buckingham Palace was bombed. He felt that he could now identify with his people and look them in the face.

Above right: High above the scene the Union Jacks flap gaily in the breeze, and in the street below this small community are determined to enjoy their street party. The event being celebrated is probably the very welcome visit of the uncrowned Edward VIII in June 1936. As usual the people of Exeter put their heart and soul into having a good time. The visit took in Exeter and Bradninch and followed an earlier local tour by Edward in 1931 when he was the Prince of Wales. On that occasion the Prince opened new extensions to the University College and inaugurated the new bypass named Prince of Wales Road.

The 1936 royal visit depicted here could have been ruined by the heavy showers experienced on the day, but local people who had turned out in their thousands long before the appointed hour of arrival would have none of it. Local newspaper reports from the time spoke of every street being a riot of bunting and flags, and how the King delighted the crowds by waving his hat as he drove past.

Both pictures: The Union Jack has been hung upside down - but who cares? Elizabeth has been crowned Queen, and mums, dads, and children alike are going to enjoy the occasion, with lots of games, music, fun and laughter *(bottom)*. In Exeter, the coronation was a great excuse for a knees-up, with dances, special shows, and fireworks displays. It was the same story across the entire country, and Britain was turned into a riot of red, white and blue. New songs were composed to celebrate the occasion - perhaps readers will remember 'Let's all be new Elizabethans'? Coronation day, 2nd June 1953, was inclined to be cool for the time of year, and persistent drizzle put a damper on many parties across Britain. However, the bare arms, summer frocks and an obvious lack of rain in these photographs makes us think that this particular party could have been held on an alternative date.

A rash of Union Jacks and paper hats demonstrated your support for the new Queen; fervent patriotism even came into the clothes worn at this street party *(below left)!* From Grandma to the youngest toddler, everyone was having the time of their life! Were these

enthusiastic partygoers lucky enough to have seen the coronation on television? Television was a novelty to the vast majority of people at the time. Although Britain had a television service as early as 1936 (suspended during the second world war), few people could afford to buy the expensive sets - and the range of programmes was very limited anyway. By the 1950s sets were beginning to get cheaper, and the Queen's Coronation presented many families with the ideal reason to buy or rent a TV set. Those who did not simply crowded into the parlours of more fortunate neighbours to watch the event! In 1960 television licences passed the ten million mark for the first time.

AROUND AND ABOUT

Christmas 1957 *saw the beginning of what was to become British tradition when the Queen made her very first television Christmas broadcast. Her grandfather King George V was the first monarch to broadcast a Christmas Day message over the radio.*

The Beatles' first *single 'Love Me Do', produced with Parlophone in 1962, turned the music scene upside down - and Decca were left kicking themselves for rejecting the 'Fab Four'. Three years later the Beatles received MBEs from the Queen.*

Loud cheers *greeted the jury's verdict when D H Lawrence's banned novel 'Lady Chatterley's Lover' was passed for general readership in 1960. The initial print-run of 200,000 copies detailing the erotic encounters of the lady and her gamekeeper sold out on the first day.*

Christmas and children go together like turkey and stuffing or holly and mistletoe. It's a magical time, peppered with fancy dress parties, visits to Santa's grotto, the writing of lists of presents wanted and the secret wrapping of little parcels for Mum and Dad. Christmas is also hard work, and even the youngest schoolchildren are not spared when it comes to learning new songs, memorising lines, trying on

costumes, practising carols, and getting as near word-perfect as possible ready for the Big Day. At last, all is ready and at nativity plays across the country, little angels don their paper wings and a diminutive Mary and Joseph find there is no room at the inn.

There was no shortage of mums and little brothers and sisters to watch this Christmas concert staged by Exeter schoolchildren back in 1951. Perhaps these mothers were partly responsible for the sewing of costumes that must have been going on behind the scenes for many weeks! Were you among this cheerful band of singers?

Bird's eye view

Grimy factories belching smoke, warehouses, mills and foundries, tiny, crowded houses; these were the conditions in which the thousands of residents of the West Quarter lived before the sweeping developments of the late 20th century. There were no such luxuries as indoor toilets, bathrooms, gas or electricity. Families from as many as half a dozen houses had to share a single water tap and a couple of toilets. Yet despite the grinding poverty there was an overall sense of community among those who lived here, and many were sad to have to leave after a lifetime spent among the noise, the inevitable rats, and the overpowering smells that rose continually from the leather tannery, the sausage skin works and the rag and bone yard. Times were hard, but unlike many cities, Exeter did not forget the less fortunate. A number of helping hands reached out to keep the wolf from many a door. The Salvation Army, for example, started their well-known Farthing Breakfast scheme, where the slightly better-off dropped in with their odd farthings to provide mugs of hot cocoa and three thick slices of bread - two of them with jam - for West Quarter children. The scheme was later adopted by the Express and Echo. The Exe Island Mission provided hot dinners, with meat, veg and potatoes heaped up for only a penny; and the Soup Kitchen in the Lower Market played an important part.

All roads lead to the bridge, the focal point of this photograph. And so much has changed since then, not least the bridge itself, which is now of course two modern bridges. In the days long before Western Way was laid down, across the bridge Bonhay Road leads off towards the left past the cattle market, and Commercial Road to the right. Fore Street Hill points diagonally upwards towards the right corner, its steep gradient strangely flattened by the angle of the shot. Buses and cars, looking like Dinky toys in a model village, are crossing the busy Exe Bridge; a single decker is turning right

The Mayor, Councillor Perry, opened the new bridge in March 1905 - he also drove the first of the new trams

into Okehampton Street. The Exe Bridge owed its existence to the coming of the electric tram system. The three-arched stone bridge which had stood there since 1778 was demolished and a new steel bridge erected in its place; at the centre, traction poles for the trams were incorporated into the design. Watched by huge crowds, the Mayor, Councillor Perry, officially opened the new bridge in March 1905. He also got to drive the first of the new trams! The last of Exeter's napier green and primrose trams - also driven by Cllr Perry - ran in 1931. Nine of the fleet were sold on to Plymouth; eight car bodies were used as garden sheds - and the last of the old trams left the depot bound for that great tram shed in the sky.

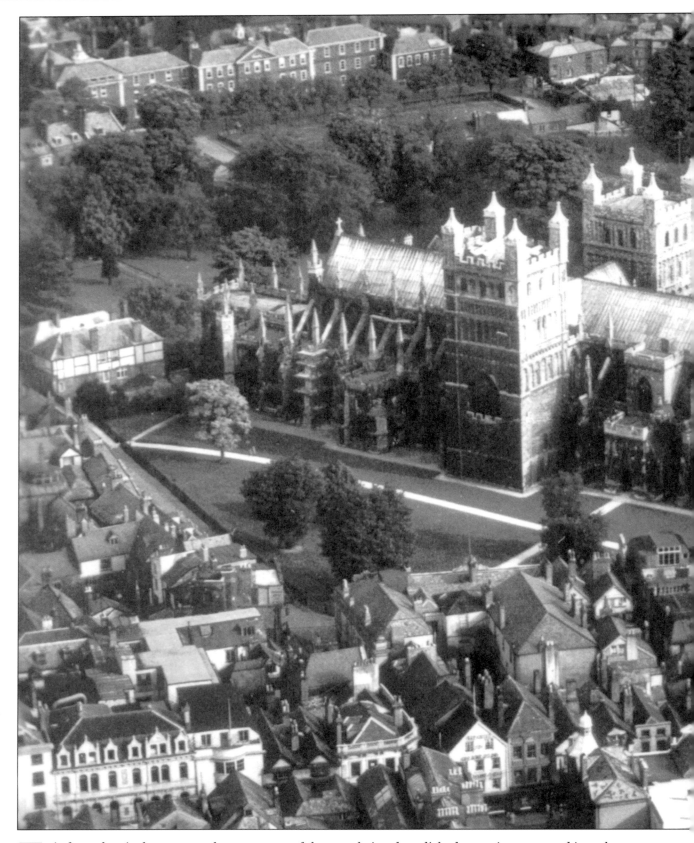

It is from the air that you get the true sense of the beauty and greatness of Exeter Cathedral, with its spires and turrets pointing upwards, reaching out towards heaven. The first Norman Cathedral was consecrated in 1133, but people worshipped God in this place for several hundred years before that. When the cathedral was enlarged in the 13th and 14th centuries, the original Norman towers, instead of being demolished, were incorporated into the new building; a lesson to be learned here, perhaps.... Further restoration work was carried out in the 18th century. Exeter cathedral survived the second world war, but not unscathed. A bomb badly damaged St James's Chapel in May 1942, but the damaged pieces were later painstakingly reassembled and restored. The cathedral is as beautiful inside as out, and the rich

history of the building can be seen in its carvings in stone and wood, its magnificent stained glass windows, the amazing but inaccurate 15th century clock depicting the earth as a golden ball with the sun moving around it, the great four manual organ, and the impressive one-and-a-half ton bishop's throne, carved in 1316 from local oak. For all its ancient history, however, Exeter Cathedral is a living church, and modern sculpture and embroidery have been incorporated into its fabric. Above all, it remains a house of worship, with daily services, music and prayer. This pre-war aerial view shows Colsons department store (now Dingles) on the High Street in the bottom left and the Victorian St Mary Major, which was taken down in the early 1970s, revealing the Roman legionary bath.

On the move

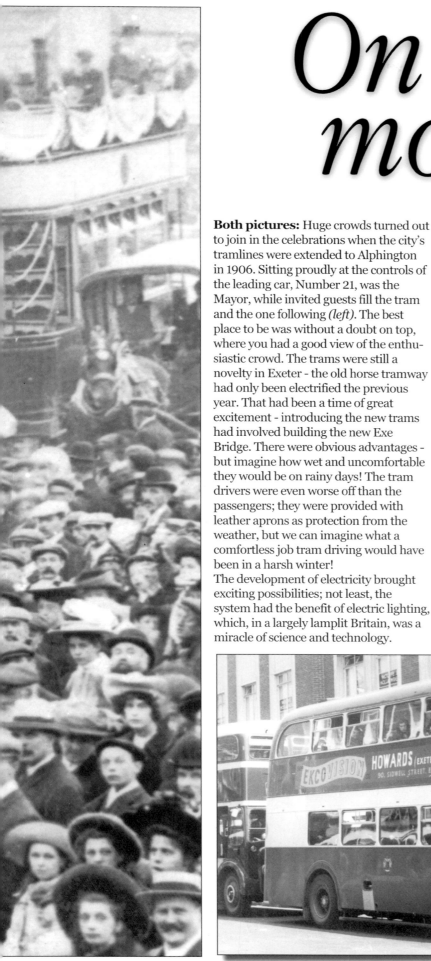

Both pictures: Huge crowds turned out to join in the celebrations when the city's tramlines were extended to Alphington in 1906. Sitting proudly at the controls of the leading car, Number 21, was the Mayor, while invited guests fill the tram and the one following *(left)*. The best place to be was without a doubt on top, where you had a good view of the enthusiastic crowd. The trams were still a novelty in Exeter - the old horse tramway had only been electrified the previous year. That had been a time of great excitement - introducing the new trams had involved building the new Exe Bridge. There were obvious advantages - but imagine how wet and uncomfortable they would be on rainy days! The tram drivers were even worse off than the passengers; they were provided with leather aprons as protection from the weather, but we can imagine what a comfortless job tram driving would have been in a harsh winter!

The development of electricity brought exciting possibilities; not least, the system had the benefit of electric lighting, which, in a largely lamplit Britain, was a miracle of science and technology.

By 1910, Britain had more than 11,000 electric trams running on two and a half thousand miles of track. Four foot eight and a half inches was adopted as the standard British gauge. The golden age of the tram lasted until the 1930s; Exeter's last tram ran on 19th August 1931.

As in so many places, Exeter's bus service began with a link between railway station and the tramway network. The London and South Western Railway introduced a motor bus service in 1904 between Queen Street station and Chagford - though there was only one bus a day. A rather better service evolved in Exeter, and the buses were ready and waiting to take over from the trams. Bus Number 58, here seen on the Crossmead route will stir memories among our readers *(below)*. The bus advertises Howards of Sidwell Street on its side panel. When they took over from the trams in 1931, buses carried no advertising. Instead, the wording on the upper panel simply read 'Exeter Corporation'. Transport enthusiasts might be interested in the fact that Number 58, a Guy Arab 6LW, was new in February 1957, and was sold on in December 1970.

Both pictures: Those of us who are old enough to remember the days when steam trains huffed into Exeter's various railway stations recall them with a pang of real nostalgia. Perhaps you were one of the enthusiastic band of train-spotting boys and girls who jotted down engine numbers in their ever-ready notebooks? For all their smoke and dirt, there can be no denying that steam trains definitely had the edge over their successors. But steam, as we know, was doomed, and the diesel and electric trains that were introduced across the country in the mid-1950s definitely lacked the character of the old steam engine. Part of the old moat at Rougemont Castle formed an unlikely site for Exeter Central - originally Queen Street Station, and piers to support the structure had to be sunk an incredible 30ft. Fire destroyed much of the station in June 1927; it was improved and extended, and the new facility, renamed Exeter Central, was declared officially open by the Mayor of Exeter in July 1933 *(right)*.

A couple of miles outside the city lay Pinhoe *(below)*, and the camera caught a member of the railway staff in a rare moment when he could spare the time to lean nonchalantly on his windowsill. What a pity we don't know his name! His would have been the very responsible task of closing the level crossing to traffic whenever a train was due - and preventing anyone in a hurry from being foolhardy enough to risk a last-minute dash for the other side. These crossing gates were replaced in 1968 by manned half-barriers - an even greater temptation to impatient motorists and pedestrians. Pinhoe station was built in 1871, and has been used by both passenger and goods trains for over 100 years.

Shopping spree

Although most readers will remember this corner as Walton's, the department store where you could get everything from a reel of cotton to a sofa, Mason's was one of Exeter's most prestigious fashion establishments, and rightly deserves a place in peoples memories. Their advertising boasted that they had 'The largest stock in the West of England of all the latest millinery novelties direct from Paris and the best London houses.' (The 1924 Exeter Guide.)

At the time, mourning clothes were immediately donned by grieving families who had lost loved ones; Mason's promised that mourning orders could be 'executed in a few hours'. Ladies' costumes, mantles, furs and the latest hats were all stocked at Mason's. This was many years before the tide of public opinion swung violently against the wearing of fur; fur was very much a fashion statement in the 1920s, and the fact that your collar was genuine was often reinforced with the head of the unfortunate animal. But faux was the way to go, and 50 years on lay the heyday of 'fun fur'. Some of our lady readers will no doubt remember with nostalgia their 'ocelot' or 'ermine'; those fake furs might have been cheap but they were not 'tacky'. Stylish and affordable, the fun to wear furs could be seen everywhere.

Above: An amazing staff of nine stand alongside the huge stock of poultry and game hanging outside Lethbridge's. Is one of these gentlemen Mr Lethbridge himself? The photograph was taken in 1927, and we can see from the number of birds on display that a chicken dinner was even more popular then than it is now - Britain was a nation of meat eaters and vegetarians were looked on as belonging to the lunatic fringe! During the 1920s and 30s, of course, your chicken was likely to have been served with sage and onion stuffing, roast potatoes and vegetables, whereas a good number of today's chicken lovers would probably choose to eat it fried, with chips, or in a good hot curry! One of Mr Lethbridge's signs, written in beautiful copperplate, emphasises his commitment to good service: 'No extra charge made for preparing or delivering to any part of the city.' The deliveries would be the task of the young lad on the right. A second sign, requesting good fowls and rabbits is aimed at local producers (and owners of shotguns).

Above right: At one time the International Stores chain had a branch in many towns and cities around the country. This branch at the top of Fore Street had an incredible staff of seven people, from the manager to the young delivery boy on the right. Small grocery chains and corner butchers were the traditional way to shop, and customers would queue to be served while the butcher cubed our stewing steak, and cut our sausages

from a long string hanging over the counter - a far cry from today's plastic packs! - and the grocer would weigh out everything, from square pats of butter to dried fruit. Does any reader remember those blue bags they used to pack the sugar in? People might have had to wait a while longer to be served, but at least they had the benefit of personal attention from the staff. Things were to remain that way until the mid-1950s, when self-service shopping began to catch on. The trend started slowly, but soon many shopkeepers found themselves installing baskets and new fixtures and going self service. It was the thin end of the wedge.

Below: 'Cycle Sale! Cycle bargains!' shouts the row of posters in the White Pearl Cycle Companies' window, in an attempt to pull in the punters who could afford to invest in a set of wheels, and three enthusiasts (one of them perhaps the proprietor of the business) take the opportunity to be recorded for posterity by the camera. Beautifully executed signs in the windows inform us that White Pearl cycles were 'fitted with Clincher tyres'. Back in 1906, £5 or £6 would buy you the latest bicycle - which seems like a real bargain until you take into account the weekly wage of a working man at the time! People who are used to living in places where the terrain is flat and the roads level would perhaps be surprised that a city with as many hills as Exeter would have so many keen cyclists. Nevertheless, cycling has been a popular sport here since the days of the penny-farthing, and the popular Exeter Cycling Club was formed as far back as 1873, making it one of the oldest clubs in Britain.

Bottom: The opportunity to have a photograph taken has caused a little excitement at Courtney & Co, St Thomas' well-known drapery store. Posing carefully in the doorway are three young assistants, uniformly dressed, probably in respectable black, as such a responsible position demanded. Even their shoes are identical, and each sports the new bobbed hair that was all the rage at the time. But these girls are not the only members of staff to be caught on camera; two young ladies on the upper sales floor are determined not to be left out, they also want a piece of the action and have

raised the sash windows on each side of the building. Courtney's was a large and popular store situated on the corner of Alphington Street. Note their rather nice sign on the corner window of the first floor, where, picked out in small panes of leaded glass, are the words 'Show Room'. A bewildering choice of goods is on show in the windows; what a pity we can't pick out exactly what is on offer. We can see, however, that the window on the right is completely filled with a wonderful array of hats. Before the mid 1940s no self-respecting woman would have been seen out of doors without a hat.

SPEND, SPEND, SPEND!

By the late 1950s our *shopping habits were being influenced by television advertising. The first TV commercials appeared on 22nd September 1955, and among the products advertised on the first day were Gibbs SR toothpaste, Cadbury's Drinking Chocolate, Dunlop tyres, Woman magazine, Lux, Surf, Shredded Wheat and Brillo.*

Post-war prosperity meant *that many working-class families could afford to buy luxury items such as refrigerators, freezers, washing machines, television sets, radiograms, and other electrical goods. Britain was on the way to becoming a consumer society.*

Refrigeration had a direct *influence on life in the 50s and 60s. Now women need not shop every day for fresh food as meat, milk and fish would keep for days longer in the fridge. Food for freezing could be bought in bulk, sparking off a whole new trend in shopping.*

The pace of modern life in *the 1960s meant that products which saved time and labour, such as heated hair rollers and pre-packaged foods, became popular. Remember 'Rael-Brook Toplin, the shirt you don't iron? And brushed nylon sheets?*

The flags mounted above Ackroyd's windows to announce the firm's sale are hardly needed. The price tickets on the goods on display speak for themselves, and the housewives of Exeter have turned out in full force in search of a bargain. Queueing has long been a way of life in Britain, and the ladies, being used to it, have formed a very orderly line. Towards the front of the queue every eye is, of course, turned on the

windows, examining the dresses, underwear, aprons and children's clothes on display - though they probably selected what they wanted to buy days before the sale began. Each lady in this hopeful line, shopping basket in hand, waits patiently for her turn. How many reached the front of the queue only to be faced with disappointment, we wonder? One older lady stands apart from the rest, gazing into the shop window. Has she missed a bargain, and is wondering if it is worth her while to join the end of the queue? The cloche hats worn low over the brow speak of the 1920s; in fact the photograph dates from July 25th 1926. To the right of the picture the old Mint Methodist Church can just be seen.

At work

This page and overleaf: What would life be like without the Royal Devon and Exeter Hospital? Swift treatment and the benefit of modern technology has become so much part of our life today that we tend to take the facilities of our hospital for granted. The Devon and Exeter was founded by the Dean of Exeter Cathedral, Alured Clarke, at the beginning of the 1740s. At the time there was not a single hospital between Bristol and Land's End, and the Dean promised one to the city. Sadly, he did not live to see the Devon and Exeter open in 1743.

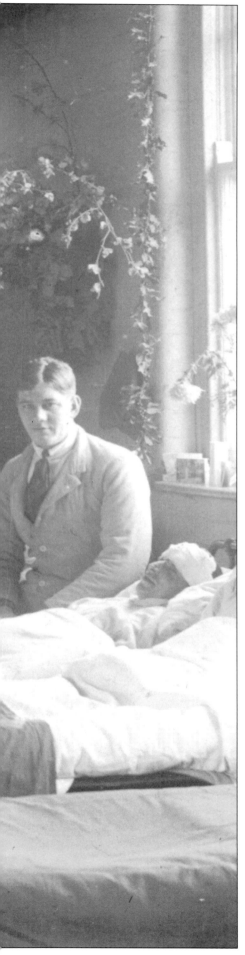

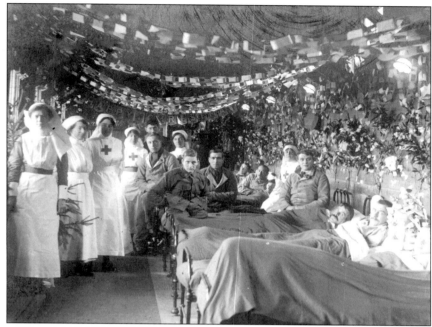

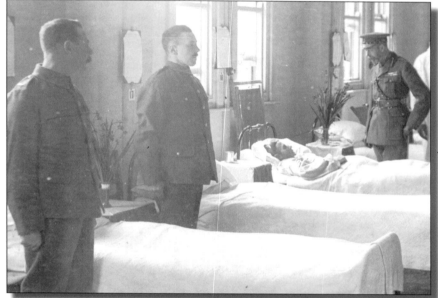

From previous page: Modern medicine was still in its infancy at the time; almost a century would pass before Edward Jenner introduced vaccination, and it was to be more than a hundred years before Lister began to fight germs with carbolic acid. The D&E moved into the forefront of new developments, however, and had their own X-ray unit as early as 1898. The following year, the Duke and Duchess of York (afterward King George V and Queen Mary) opened a new wing at the hospital, after which Queen Victoria allowed the addition of the word 'Royal' to its title. Those were the days when the medical challenges to be faced were polio, TB, osteomyelitis and rickets. During World War I, wounded soldiers found healing and peace at the RD&E; some of them were fortunate enough to be able to meet the King, photographed during his second visit to Exeter in September 1915 *(above)*. Readers will remember that even as recently as the 1940s and 50s hospitals were highly regimented, and Sister ruled supreme over every neat and tidy ward! Things had obviously changed little from the wartime years, when even the Christmas festivities pictured here brought very little relaxation of Matron's rules! The RD & E moved to the city's outskirts in the 1970s.

The manufacture of success and the machinations of progress!

Hardinge Machine Tools Limited was established in the United Kingdom in the year 1937. However, the history of the company does in fact go as far back as 1890. It was on the 23rd of July that year when Hardinge Machine Tools Limited's parent company, Hardinge Brothers Incorporated, came into existence.

Two Canadian brothers, Franklin and Henry Hardinge decided to join forces and use their combined experience to establish their own business. Franklin, who had served his apprenticeship as a watchmaker, had subsequently invented and designed several watchmaker's tools. The brothers business was set up to manufacture these precision devices. They began work in a tiny, eight foot square factory, in the rear of a boarding house at 359 West Monroe Street in Chicago. The brothers were soon manufacturing the finest bench lathes of the time, as well as producing the first 'true' lathe chucks, and their company began to make its mark on the industrial world. Indeed, by 1938, they were able to merge their burgeoning enterprise with Morrison Machine Products, manufacturers of precision collets to become Hardinge Brothers Incorporated. A collet is a device for gripping components for machining, so the two company's products were totally complementary.

It was only a year before the merger reached completion, in 1937, that the brothers decided to create a manufacturing base for their collets and associated tooling in the United

Kingdom. In fact Hardinge Brothers had already been selling lathes and equipment in this country for several years through a well known British machine tool firm, Alfred Herbert. It was one of Herbert's directors, Jamie Blair, who introduced Douglas Anderson, the person assigned to the

Below: *Hardinge's Elmira premises in the 1930s.*
Bottom and facing page top: *The demonstration lorry in 1952 - an old war time ambulance which had been converted and reinforced to house the demonstration machines, including the one on the left - the HLV Centre Lathe. This lorry was the site of many comical scenes between Ted Shipman and Roy Bradbury who tried to frighten each other, seeing who would go the furthest to test the lorry's suspension!*

were to be based for the next 34 years. The early 1940s brought rapid growth for Hardinge Machine Tools as the company played a substantial part in the war effort necessitating the building of a completely new factory and offices two miles away at a green field site in Hanworth. With orders in excess of 450 pieces a day, it soon became necessary to open a further satellite factory in Acton to cope with the heavy demand for munitions until the cessation of hostilities in 1945. During these hectic war years, Hardinge Machine Tools actually increased its workforce from the initial six to a total of 400 employees!

Business continued to boom and by the late 1940s, Hardinge Machine Tools was in a healthy place in the industry selling Hardinge American-built lathes and large quantities of UK-manufactured collets and feedfingers. It was at this point that the parent Corporation made the decision to

Above left: *A 1950s van loaded with Hardinge products.* ***Below:*** *Hardinge lathes on show at a machine tool exhibition in Paris during the 1950s.*

task of finding a suitable manufacturer, to Automotive Engineering Ltd. This company, established in 1917, was manufacturing general engineering products and automobile pistons in South West London when Doug Anderson paid it a visit.

Automotive Engineering Limited seized the opportunity to work for Hardinge Brothers and began manufacturing their collets, Style B feedfingers and form tools. This then marked the commencement of Hardinge Machine Tools Limited in the United Kingdom. The new company emerged from humble beginnings, to say the least! Indeed, initially it employed only six people who worked from a corner of one of Automotive Engineering's workshops

The fledgling company soon began to take flight as Britain's rearmament programme gathered momentum. By the year 1939, they were successful enough to be able to move to premises in Feltham at which core management and sales

expand the product range in Britain, giving permission for the HLV Centre Lathe to be built at the Feltham factory. Incorporating several advanced features, this new machine quite literally became the subject of a major sales drive, being taken all over Europe in a specially adapted demonstration vehicle - a converted ex-wartime Bedford ambulance. The sophisticated HLV, sold in very large numbers, particularly to Britain's leading precision manufacturers in the aerospace, avionics, electrical and scientific industries. Interestingly, the company fixed the price for the HLV at £1,000, this being based, not on what it cost to make, but on what the market was prepared to pay for a machine of such capability. A turret lathe version, the HC model, was also built at Feltham and became equally as popular for bigger batch production of high precision work.

In 1962, Hardinge opened a factory on Marsh Barton in Exeter, taking advantage of favourable regional development conditions to set up a supplementary component manufacturing facility. When in 1973 the land on which the Feltham factory stood was designated for residential development, the Exeter factory became the bridgehead for a complete move to Marsh Barton.

The 1980s was a decade filled with change for Hardinge Machine Tools. In 1982, the parent corporation, Hardinge Brothers Incorporated, acquired the 51 per cent UK owned shareholding which by then had passed from Automotive Engineering to Sheepbridge Engineering and then to the giant engineering group, GKN. The following year, a prototype American designed numerically controlled centre lathe, the HXL was put into production at Exeter as a successor to the HLV-H. This was at an uncertain time in the general evolution of machine tools, when rapid developments in electronics technology were precipitating many new machine configurations and control system possibilities. The HXL and its later marque, the computerised HXL-S, were well-engineered and extremely accurate, but their centre lathe configuration failed to attract mass orders in the

same way as the slantbed format; a more market orientated approach which was then successfully adopted for the Hardinge 'Talent' lathe. This involved collaboration with a Japanese manufacturer, Akebono, who built the main machine elements in Tokyo and then shipped them to Exeter for assembly. The Talent sold well and created an important foothold for Hardinge in the wider general precision lathe market. But sales of other Exeter built models were falling and it became more viable economically to import Hardinge's American built machines. Consequently, the UK factory was closed and the Exeter base became the Head Office of a purely sales and service operation for the UK and Europe.

Then, in 1993, the US corporate Chairman and CEO, Bob Agan, set a new direction for the corporation announcing, 'Hardinge will be a leading provider of machine tools to the world-wide metal cutting marketplace'. This represented a fundamental change in policy involving the manufacture of

Top: The interior of the factory in the early 1960s.
Below: The sales office at Exeter during the 1960s.

Looking back at the last 110 years of Hardinge history, it is interesting to consider how the company has grown with the increasing need for precision machined parts. Today, instead of just making parts for watches, Hardinge machines are producing components for space vehicles, jet engines, cars, computers, surgical instruments, optical instruments - in fact - for almost every sphere of modern industrial production. Virtually every aircraft flying in the western world today is held together with parts made in the UK on Hardinge lathes, and many of the leading Formula One racing cars and engines are manufactured using Hardinge machines. Even the world's fastest car, the supersonic Thrust SSC, was built with parts machined on a Hardinge lathe.

If Franklin and Henry Hardinge were to visit their company today they would surely be amazed at the capability of the latest multiple axis computerised lathes, consistently accurate within a twentieth of a human hair's breadth. However, they would no doubt, still recognise the same innovative thought and entrepreneurial spirit in evidence that they themselves used to found the business in 1890.

Above left: The Matford Park premises today. Top right: A modern distribution lorry. Top left: The opening of the Matford Park premises. Pat Ervin, USA Executive Vice President on the left and Bob Duxbury, Managing Director, on the right. Below: World land speed record holding car, Thrust SSC, under construction at G Force in 1996.

all types of metal cutting machines; not just the small 'Super-Precision' lathes for which Hardinge had been well known since the 1890s. Furthermore, the company would have to provide a broader variety of machine sizes and prices to attract a wider range of customers. It was not long before the corporation accomplished these goals, emerging in the late 1990s as a successful global manufacturer of lathes, grinders and machining centres, with factories in Switzerland, Taiwan and China, as well as an expanded manufacturing plant in Elmira, New York State. Indeed, by 1999, Hardinge Incorporated (as it is now known) achieved an annual turnover of 250 million US dollars.

Meanwhile, here in Exeter. Hardinge Machine Tools Limited has flourished, in 1997 financing the building of a new £1.5 million purpose designed premises with superb training and demonstration facilities at Matford Park. The expanded product range now incorporates Kellenberger CNC (computer numerically controlled) cylindrical grinders and a wide range of Hardinge CNC lathes and vertical machining centres. The use of Hardinge machines is now as widespread in the UK as it is in the USA, the Hardinge name now being a byword for quality machine tools on both sides of the Atlantic.

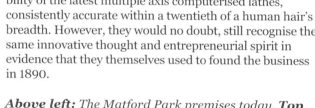

Tailoring business to suit the people of Exeter

The interesting history of Thomas Moore of Exeter Limited, the family-run department store company, can be traced back as far as 1907. It was in this year that Thomas Moore opened his first shop. Thomas had built up his knowledge of the men's outfitting trade in Bristol and London. However, when he moved to Exeter with his parents, to live in Belmont Road, he decided to put his knowledge to use and set up his own business.

On March 21st, 1907 Thomas opened his shop at 103 Fore Street as an up-to-date, 'Gentleman's Hosier, Hatter and Tailor'. The shop was located in the less affluent area of Exeter and as a result Thomas decided to provide the best possible value for money for his range of goods which he promised were, 'unsurpassed for variety, quality and style'! Indeed, his top quality made-to-measure suits were sold for just 35 shillings!

The new business was a success with the locals and it wasn't long before its reputation spread to the more affluent sections of Exeter society! Thomas was an enterprising man, and soon moved into the larger premises next door, and became one of the first to install gas lighting to illuminate his shop front, as the picture below shows, circa 1910. He was soon able to introduce a range of children's wear to his shop. Indeed, he employed an early marketing technique by giving penknives away to his customers. He did however, make a nominal charge of ha'penny for them, so as to fend off bad luck! Thomas was also a local pioneer of motorcycling and he took pleasure in riding his Triumph machine around the streets of Exeter.

It was his love of motorcycles that led Thomas to join the army as a despatch rider at the outbreak of the first world war. However, it was the advent of the war that brought tragedy for the Moores. Sadly, the 34 year old Thomas was killed in 1917 at Lillebeck, in one of the last big battles of the war. Thomas' bereaved mother, Sophia, had been running her son's business in his absence but on hearing the news of his death decided to sell the shop. Thomas' memory has however, been honoured ever since by the subsequent

Above left: Thomas Moore in a picture dating from 1914. *Below:* The premises around 1910.

owners of the business who have continued to run it in his name. Indeed, the name Thomas Moore can also be found on the war memorial on the wall of St Olave's Church opposite the shop.

In 1952 the new partnership of Edward Walters and Ralph Alford formed to run Thomas Moore of Exeter. Under their guidance, the business flourished quite dramatically. Only two years later the partners were able to purchase the credit traders, Wonnacotts. Wonnacotts' staff and customers were transferred to Fore Street and the business was given a new name, Thomas Moore and Wonnacott Limited. Although the credit side of the business expanded the new name was eventually dropped after a couple of years.

During the 1960s the expansion of the business continued. The increased public interest in fashion wear meant that a girls and a ladies wear range could be added to the shop. The success of these new ranges allowed the business to continue in its expansion and development. The number of people employed by the company also increased, and in 1974 Thomas Moore became one of the first companies in Exeter to be awarded the coveted Distributive Training Award.

The year 1982 was a year of mixed emotions for the company. Edward Walters died in this, the same year in which the company celebrated its 75th anniversary. His son Michael succeeded him in the business joining Ralph's sons, Norman and Philip, in running the company, until

Thos. Moore,

HOSIER,
HATTER,
TAILOR.

New Season's Fashions.
Perfect Fit and Style
Guaranteed

THE UNIVERSAL SHIRT,
2 6

103, Fore Street,
EXETER.

his retirement in 1998. Together they continued to make a success of the business. Indeed, in 1986, the Cavendish Furniture Store was purchased, doubling the selling space to nearly 9,000 square feet!

By 1996, the company occupied not only the original shop at 103 Fore Street, but also the two adjoining ones. The number of employees had also grown by now from the initial three, to a total of thirty five. Indeed, the third generation of Alford's, Philip's son, Stephen, joined the company in 1996.

A year later, in his role as a retained fireman, Stephen was called out to tackle a fire in Fore Street. Luckily, the fire was not at Thomas Moore, but next door. However, its stock was partially damaged by smoke. This turned out to be a blessing in disguise as when prices were cut by 25 percent the store became busier than ever, even experiencing queues out of the door!

Although the Alfords cannot, because of inflation, manage to match Thomas' prices, they do offer the same value for money that he worked to achieve in 1907. Indeed, if Thomas were able to visit the Thomas Moore department store today, he would no doubt be reassured to find that the company is managing to tailor its business to suit the people of Exeter as it always has, and always hopes to do in the future!

Above: *Early advertising.*
Below: *Today's Fore Street premises.*

Building better conditions

Whilst working as a GP in Exeter in the 1920s, Dr Lovely was horrified to see the conditions in which many people had to live. Indeed, he stated that many people were, 'condemned to exist in the dark, rat-infested miserable courts and alleys of our city'. In 1926, with a view to improving these conditions, Dr Lovely gathered together a group of affluent Exeter residents and persuaded them to lend their money very cheaply in order to re-house families from the slum areas of Exeter.

Dr Lovely's persuasions were successful and The Exeter Workmen's Dwellings Company Limited was established at Bedford Circus (now Bedford Street). Initially, finance was raised by the issue of £1 shares to members of the public interested in improving, according to an article in the Devon and Exeter Gazette, the 'insanitary, unwholesome, airless, sunless' conditions of those people living in the slum areas, mainly in the West Quarter of Exeter.

The Company began work almost immediately on the overriding condition that, for each family housed from the slums the Local Authority had to give an assurance that

their former home would be demolished. The first project undertaken by the Company was the erection of 30 three bedroom houses at Looe Road (St David's) and it was funded, like many of the pre-war projects, by loans with the Guardian Royal Exchange. This project was followed with the provision of low interest loans from The Great Western Railway Society for the erection of 50 houses at Mildmay Close, Foxhayes Road and Clayton Road, on the condition that only railway employees were accepted for these tenancies.

Indeed, by the outbreak of the second world war in 1939, the Company had managed to build a total of 550 houses and flats as part of its slum clearance scheme in Exeter. Sadly, the advent of the second world war brought with it tragedy for the city of Exeter. In 1942,

Above: Notices of events, issued by the company in the 1930s. Below: The opening of Cherry Barton by Board members on 29th December 1969.

the centre of the city was attacked by enemy aircraft and razed to the ground by explosives and incendiary bombs. As well as managing to destroy all the remaining slums, these attacks also resulted in many of their inhabitants losing their lives. Another consequence of the attacks was the destruction of the Company's offices and in 1942 it relocated to its current premises in Southernhay East.

Another far-reaching effect of the war was the passing of the Rent Restriction Act in 1939. This meant that the low rents set by the Company were frozen, with disastrous consequences. The income from rents was not even sufficient to carry out essential maintenance, resulting in years of forced neglect and the threat of the new housing

Above: *The demolition of Countess Wear School, the new site for 46 houses and flats.*
Top: *Refurbishement work at Cherry Barton in 1999.*

rapidly becoming the slums of the future! The Company was forced to sell 40 of its houses in the early 50s to raise the capital for repairs and at this time it set up its own Direct Labour Force for such works. This was to become a unique feature of the organisation that has gone from strength to strength.

In 1954 the Association ceased to be a Company when it was granted Charitable Status and was accordingly renamed, The Exeter Housing Society. Finally, in 1957 the Rent Restriction Act was ended allowing rent increases to be implemented. Although the financial struggles of the Society were not eradicated until the introduction of Fair Rents in 1970, an inspection of all 500 properties and the implementation of a long term improvement programme helped to ease the problems.
The Society continued to purchase, build and convert properties in the ensuing years and in 1981 the Church Housing Association transferred 38 properties valued at £1 million to the Society.

The Society celebrated its 70th anniversary in 1996, by which time it owned over 800 properties. Whilst the refurbishment of its existing stock continues to be important, it has also been able to once again turn its attention to new developments. One project of particular merit was the development of the former police station at Peel Row in Whipton village. This scheme of nine houses was constructed by the Society's own team which is now one of the largest employers of building labour in Exeter and has a turnover in excess of £1 million.

As it entered the new millennium the Society embarked on one of its biggest ever projects, with the construction by a local developer of 46 houses and flats on the site of the former Countess Wear First School. If Dr Lovely was able to see the housing provided by the Society today, he would be impressed rather than horrified at residents' living conditions. However, the Society is not content to rest on its laurels and is aware of the continuing need to retain affordable rents and first class services for the people of Exeter.

A driving force in Exeter

Noel Kastner was living abroad when he made the important decision to move to Britain and set up his own business. This decision was paramount to the existence of the successful company, Kastner Volvo, as it is known today.

It was in the year 1961 that Noel Kastner moved to Honiton in East Devon. Here, he took the first steps towards establishing his own business when he bought a Ford retail motor business, based in Honiton, from a Mr Sammy Tremaine. This event marked the foundation of the Kaster business name which was to remain enduring throughout the various developments and changes experienced in the company's history.

Noel immediately set to work building up his new business. Whilst operating as a Ford main dealer, the foremost aspects that the business was involved in were; service and repair and vehicle sales. Noel was assisted by two family members in his initial work to construct a successful venture. Peter Munn and Tommy Higson, Noel's son-in-laws, both joined their father-in-law in his new business. Peter worked as the Sales Manager whilst Tommy worked as the Bodyshop Manager.

The family's hard work eventually paid off and the business began to flourish. Indeed, in 1970, only nine years after its foundation, the business was in a healthy position and ready and able to expand. It was in this year that Noel made the important acquisition of a Volvo franchise. Subsequently, the business also acquired its current, long standing name, Kastner Volvo.

Kastner Volvo operated in Honiton for five years, until 1975. It was in this year that the Volvo franchise holder in Exeter, based at Bedford Street Garage, made the decision not to renew its contract with Volvo. This decision provided Noel Kastner with an exciting opportunity and one which he was happy to seize. The Exeter territory was offered to Kastner Volvo on the condition that it agreed to relocate from its premises in Honiton. This condition was met and after 14 years in Honiton, Kastner Volvo relocated to new premises in Magdalen Road, Exeter.

Initially, the new premises in Exeter were to be used for sales, service, and parts. The forecourt was also put into active use as a place from which to sell BP petrol. With the help of the company's employees, now totalling six, the business continued to thrive. The company's founder however, after accomplishing what he had set out to achieve, was ready, once again, to move on. After managing to sell his company, the site and its franchise to an Investment Company, Noel Kastner brought about the end of an era and emigrated to Australia!

Under the control of the Investment Company, Kastner Volvo continued to succeed. In fact, the rate at which the Company expanded and developed actually increased. More Volvo sites were acquired at Plymouth,

Below: *The premises in Magdalen Road.*

before, the business continued to flourish, still operating under the Kastner name.

Eventually, another branch of the business was opened in Barnstaple and the Exeter business was relocated to a new purpose built site at Matford Park. The previous site at Longbrook Terrace was redeveloped as housing, whilst the Magdalen Road site was sold for property development purposes. Indeed, in March 1999 when Ford bought Volvo cars of Sweden, the circle from Ford in Honiton, to Volvo and back to Ford was completed!

Today, the Kastner name is synonymous for Volvo in Exeter and indeed, throughout Devon. With the help of six of the Company's loyal employees, who between them have given a total of 180 years service to the business, the Company will no doubt continue to succeed, maintaining its status as a driving force throughout Devon.

Above left: *From left to right: Bob Broom (Kastner director), Malcolm Wade (Volvo), Gerry Keaney (Volvo MD), Rob Thomas (Volvo), Peter Rogers (Kastner MD), Robin Carr (Kastner director), Colin Hamman (Kastner director).* ***Top:*** *A presentation to long service employees.* ***Below:*** *The Matford Park premises today.*

Chippenham, Bristol and Bracknell and further franchises were obtained including; Rover, Renault, Toyota and BMW. By the year 1983, the Exeter business had become so successful that further developments were implemented. The increase in sales at the Exeter site meant that the forecourt had to be closed in order to make space for additional used car sales. It was also in this year that the Company acquired further premises, located at Longbrook Terrace in the heart of Exeter. Indeed, these new premises facilitated the expansion of the service and parts operation of the business.

Three years later, in 1986, Kastner Volvo had something else to celebrate along with its success and progress. It was in this year that the Company reached a significant landmark in its history and was able to celebrate its 25th anniversary in business!

In the year, 1992, the Company changed hands once again. This time, the new owners acquired the Company following a management buy-out from the receivers of the Investment Company that had originally purchased the business from Noel Kastner. As

A *friendly learning experience*

The West of England School, as it is now known, was founded in 1838 by a group of local people led by Mrs Friend. Mrs Friend had previously been instructing six blind children in portions of the gospels and recognised the need for a specialist school.

The school was established as The West of England Institute for the Instruction and Employment of the Blind and held at rooms located in South Street, Exeter. During the first year, the pupils at the school experimented with several different reading techniques. This resulted in the use of stenographic characters and raised Roman capitals.

With the help of public donations, as well as local doctors and clergy encouraging blind people to attend the school, the new establishment began to flourish. In 1840 the school moved to Paul Street where basket making and stocking-knitting was introduced to the curriculum and the first teacher was employed for 12 shillings a week!

Two years later, the school had out grown the rooms in Paul Street and consequently, moved to a donated house on St David's Hill where it was based until 1965. During the following decade the school's music teacher invented a raised form of music notation, some pupils started to learn piano tuning, and physical education and Braille were introduced. In 1893 a school room was built to accommodate 20 boys and 20 girls and by 1911, this number had risen to 70 children and 12 adults!

In 1944, as the result of an Education Act, stipulating that blind and partially sighted children should be educated separately, the school changed its name to the West of England School for the Partially Sighted and all blind children went to Bristol Blind School. It was not until 1965 that the school moved to its present sight at Countess Wear and became known as The West of England School for Children with Little or no Sight.

Today, the school is a non-maintained special school and a registered charity and comprises a Nursery, Main School, College and Specialist Department, St David's House, for young people with additional complex needs. Indeed, with its specialist teachers, small class sizes, Braille and large print resources, therapy and independent living and mobility training, the school continues, in its over 150 year tradition, to provide all the support and guidance a blind or partially sighted child will need to reach their full potential.

Above: Braille is taught from a very early age. **Below:** *The Duchess of Kent on an official visit in the early 1990s.*

A sympathetic service

The independent family Funeral Directors, M. Sillifant & Sons, has been providing a personal, confidential and caring service to the residents of Exeter since 1906, although it has not always been known by this name. It was in this year that the cabinet maker Harry Bidgood made the decision to change professions. His ambition to acquire his own business and work for himself, combined with his experience and expertise in the trade of cabinet making led him to found a Funeral Director's business.

With the help of his wife and daughters, Harry established his new business at Lansdowne Terrace in St Leonards, Exeter. Only four years later, by 1910, the business had become successful enough to be able to move to improved premises at 19/20 Holloway Street in Exeter where it continued to flourish. Indeed, M Sillifant & Sons operates from these premises to this day.

The advent of the first, and subsequently the second world wars brought with them a period of difficulty for the firm. During the war years, the business continued as usual, but Harry suffered the misfortune of seeing his workshop destroyed and his home damaged when they were hit by a bomb. To make matters worse, acting on government instructions Harry had placed 50 coffins in storage at his premises and these too were destroyed! Despite these difficulties Harry managed to maintain the business until he sold it to the Sillifant family in 1948. In accordance with Harry's wishes, they continued to run the business as an independent family concern under the new name, M. Sillifant & Sons. Muriel Sillifant became the owner and Business Manager, Uncle Bill worked as the Funeral Director, and Muriel and her husband Henry's sons and daughter also worked in the business: Gordon aged 21, Phyllis aged 17 and Bernard aged 15.

Business prospered and Muriel was able to retire in 1969 leaving Bernard and Gordon as partners. Gordon himself retired in 1986, leaving Bernard and his son Martin, the third generation of Sillifants to run the family business, as partners. M. Sillifant & Sons continues to serve the people of Exeter with the expertise, personal attention and compassion that Harry instituted all those years ago in 1906.

Above left: *'Uncle Bill', who worked alongside Harry Bidgood and then with Muriel Sillifant.*
Above right: *Bernard Sillifant.*
Below: *Bernard and Martin Sillifant with a new Daimler purchased in 1990 to add to the fleet.*

Everyone loves a parade - especially if there is a band to keep everyone in step, and people came out en masse to view this one, forming a tightly-packed crowd along the route. This photograph was taken in Sidwell Street in the year 1936.

Acknowledgments

Hazel Harvey
Mavis Piller of Exeter Postcard Society
Alan Winn of The Photographers Centre
David Fisher of Exmouth

Thanks are also due to
Peggy Burns who penned the editorial text
and Ann Ramsdale for her copywriting skills